sticks & stones

"

Words kill, words give life;
they are either poison or fruit –
you choose.

"

(Proverbs 18:21 MSG)

MICAH DAVIDSON

real life.
PUBLISHING

Published in Austin, Texas, by Real Life.

Cover photo by Keagan Henman. Unless otherwise noted, Scripture quotations are from the *Holy Bible, New Living Translation.* © 1996. Used by permission of Tyndale House Publishers, Inc., Wheaton, Illinois 60189. All rights reserved.

ISBN: 978-0-9600639-0-1 Paperback
ISBN: 978-0-9600639-1-8 eBook
First Edition printed 2019

We hope you hear from the Holy Spirit and receive God's blessings from this book by Micah Davidson and Real Life. We want to provide the highest quality resources that take the messages, music, and media of Real Life Church to the world.

Printed in the United States of America

CONTENTS

"

Sticks and stones
may break my bones,
but words will never
hurt me.

"

(Anonymous)

PREFACE

"Sticks and stones may break my bones, but words will never hurt me." This sounds good, but the reality is we all carry wounds from words that hurt us. Words do not cause bruises or actual broken bones, but they do cause emotional pain and harm. However, the good news is that words can also bring life. With our words, we can choose to heal instead of hurt, and this reality gives you more power than you can possibly imagine.

When I recently taught this message series called Sticks and Stones, I had no idea it would take on book form. We received so much positive feedback about how helpful and life-changing the series was from our campuses in Austin, Corpus Christi and those who connect with us online. My mom suggested my messages be turned into a book to impact others like it did the listeners on those encouraging Sunday mornings at Real Life. Thank you, mom!

I am humbled and grateful to present to you the result of many people working extremely hard to make this idea a reality.

This project would not have been possible without the talent of dedicated men and women God has placed around me. I would like to thank Colonel Matt Elledge for his consistent motivation and inspiration. I would like to thank Pastor Cynthia Lopez for her gifts of administration and her team for keeping me on task. I would like to thank Pastor Ali Davidson for the cover artwork and helping me edit this manuscript. I would like to thank Mary Elliott for believing that this needed to happen and the countless hours she spent writing, editing, and listening to a pastor who talks too fast and speaks in run-on sentences. Also, I would like to thank the elders of Real Life for their steadfast faithfulness, prayers and consistent words of encouragement to me. The elders of Real Life are true warriors who use their words to protect their pastor and promote God's purpose for His church.

This content, like all my messages, is not an academic pursuit to intellectually exhaust a topic, but rather a personal struggle to apply what I have learned from the Bible to my life. I have in no way mastered this topic, but I have observed the power of words in my own relationships. I am convinced that because I wrestle to be intentional with my words, there is unconditional love in my own family, supernatural strength in my friendships, an unshakeable faith among our church leaders and a God-given harmony among our church family.

The most powerful word you will ever receive is God's Word. Each morning, I read the Bible and I experience the healing power of God's Word in my own weakness, brokenness and struggle. I am thankful that God's Word never breaks our bones, but rather always heals our hearts when we are humble and honest with Him. This is why this book is filled with verses from the Scriptures that bring the life we all need. Each Bible verse is God's Word reminding us that our words are powerful and should be life-giving.

I would like to dedicate this book to my dad whose constant affirmation and prayers made me the man I am today. He always aimed his words to help others and point people to Jesus. Even though he moved to heaven last year, his encouraging words continue to echo in my heart.

– Micah Davidson

PREFACE

"

Your love for one another will prove to the world that you are my disciples.

"

(John 13:35)

INTRODUCTION

Encourage one another and build each other up,
just as in fact you are doing.
(*1 Thessalonians 5:11*)

If you are a Christian – your job is to encourage. You can't decline this calling or make excuses for not showing up to work every day. My prayer is that this book will make your job easier by giving you practical ways to be uplifting and life-giving with your words.

As I write this, our church is blessed to be growing tremendously. I believe one of the key factors of this amazing growth is that Real Life is an encouraging place to be! We actually encourage each other! We love each other! Jesus said this is the greatest indicator that we were His followers: *Your love for one another will prove to the world that you are my disciples.* (*John 13:35*)

Imagine that! A church that loves each other and builds

each other up. I am convinced that as we continue to unconditionally love each other, lift each other up in prayer, and encourage each other with life-giving words, it is inevitable that our church will continue to grow.

People are attracted to good news and positive words. Why? Because, we live in a negative, cynical world filled with conflict and cutdowns. Been on Twitter lately? Face it, we live in a world of people who are desperate for encouragement. As we continue to choose to build up rather than tear down, be generous rather than selfish, to strengthen our relationships rather than kill them, we will continue to reap the blessings that God has planned for us.

Choose to encourage people with your words and you will change your life.

Have you ever been to a church that is filled with negativity and discouragement? Most churches I have been to, big or small, in the city or the country, are filled with nice people who genuinely love God and love each other. However, I have been to churches that slid into a negative rut. It can happen because churches are made up of people and they form a holy huddle, create an "us four and no more" mentality with a cynical, condemning attitude toward outsiders.

Churches are trying to figure out why no one is coming. Many times, they'll find they are a church that is not intentional with their words. Because churches are made up of people, a church can become full of complainers, gossipers, negative and judgmental people. This type of attitude is contagious and can spread throughout the church family and even affect the church staff.

It's like the story I heard recently about an elderly lady coming into the worship center one morning. A staff person greets her, exuding an attitude that he did not want to be there that day, and says, "Ma'am, can I help you find a seat?

The older lady said, "Yes, please. I want to sit on the front row."

The greeter offers, "Ma'am, you don't want to sit on the front row. Our pastor's sermons are so bad and so boring, you are going to fall asleep, and you don't want to fall asleep on the front row."

The lady replied, "Young man, do you know who I am?" To which he answered, "No."

She then replied, "I am the pastor's mother."

The astonished staff member said, "Well ma'am, do you know who I am?"

When she said, "No," he quickly threw out a, "Good!" and took off!

I am so thankful this doesn't happen at Real Life! My mom sits on the second row, not the front row. Seriously, I am thankful that Real Life is made up of so many people who are committed to the ministry of encouragement and the ministry of loving people where they are, accepting people for who they are, to seeing people for not where they are but where they can be. It is so refreshing to be part of a church family committed to building people up.

Here is the reality: there are some habits we need to *stop* when it comes to words and some patterns we need to *start*. This book will help with both just like this verse says ...

> (STOP) *Do not let any unwholesome talk come out of your mouths,* (START) *but only what is helpful for building others up according to their needs, that it may benefit those who listen.*
> *(Ephesians 4:29)*

This is an easy verse to read, but if we are honest, very difficult to actually apply. Let this sink in, think about this. Your words have the power to build up, the power to bless, the power to help. Before you say a word – you should think about what is going to help – what is going to benefit others.

How do you do this? How do you become so intentional, so careful with your words that you actually encourage everyone who listens to you? How are you going to stop saying certain things and start using your words differently? This is what we will unpack and discover together in the following pages.

As a Christian, your job is to encourage. Each chapter of this book is designed to be relevant and real with the struggles we all face to be helpful with our words while offering simple, yet powerful steps to do your job more effectively and intentionally.

Let's get started ...

"

Words kill, words give life;
they are either poison or fruit –
you choose.

"

(Proverbs 18:21 MSG)

1

A WORD TO THE WISE

One morning last week, I was in a big hurry, rushing around when I remembered that I needed to check the mailbox. I slipped on my shoes quickly and hustled out the door. After a few steps, massive pain hit my foot – specifically, my big toe – it was excruciating! Stopped me in my tracks. The quicker I could get my shoe off, the better. I kicked it off, and you would not believe what crawled out.

A Texas-sized scorpion.

Have you seen Texas scorpions? It felt like it was two feet long! My toe hurt ALL day – I could feel my pulse in my foot for hours. I'm not a wimp, but it was so painful and came out of nowhere. It hurt.

Have you ever been stung by a scorpion or a bee? Do you remember where you were when it happened? It came out of nowhere, and it was probably painful, right?

Words.

Did you know that is exactly how words are? They can hurt, too. You weren't expecting it, but all of the sudden somebody says something and it stings. All of the sudden you open up your email and somebody's got a special gift for you. They just kind of verbally threw up all over you, and what they said is very painful. You opened up Facebook and someone left a post. It's cryptic, but you know it's about you. Or someone tweets something negative about you and all of the sudden, your day changes. Words cause pain.

Have you ever been hurt or stung by someone's words?

Listen, I'm not signing up for a scorpion sting every day, but I can tell you this. A little bit of baking soda, a little bit of Benadryl, the sting goes away and I can't even feel it anymore. But words? I would much rather get stung by a scorpion than by some of the things people have said to me. Some of you can remember something that somebody said to you years ago, and it still stings. It still hurts. You can remember the email, the post, the words that were said. 'You'll never amount to anything.' 'You'll never measure up.' Whatever the words were that caused that hurt are still there. Words. Are. Powerful.

As we walk through this book together, let's evaluate our words. Are they positive, or negative? Specifically, are they positive or negative in our relationships? God designed us to say positive and uplifting words and He also designed us to run on the positive and uplifting words of others. I don't care how great the relationship looks on the outside – if you aren't pouring the right words into it; if you are not communicating the way God intended for us to; it's going to go downhill. Quickly.

Our nation needs some positive words. Our entire country needs a total re-boot. Now look at these stats: 50% of wives say, "My husband doesn't talk to me like I'd like for him to.'" In 86% of divorces, the statement was made that one of the major reasons for the divorce was, "We just couldn't communicate."² In America, one in four kids says, "I've never had a significant conversation with my dad."³ Obviously, everyone needs some help. Let's look to the Bible (God's Word) to help us with our words.

Let's start with James 3. Words are so important in relationships that James spends almost all of this chapter talking about how to use words. As we walk through this chapter in James, we are going to notice three things about words in the first three verses.

1. We will all give an account for our words.

Did you know that? Whatever you have said – texted – tweeted – posted – emailed, you will have to answer to God for your words. That is a pretty sobering thought, and is what James is saying. Look at how he starts:

> *Dear brothers and sisters, not many of you should become teachers in the church, for we who teach will be judged more strictly.* (James 3:1)

Why is James jumping on teachers right out of the gate here? Why is he picking on pastors? One reason is that teachers and pastors use a LOT of words. And those words, like all words, influence other people. Teachers speak, we listen. So James is pointing out that every pastor, every teacher, will be held accountable for what they say.

That is serious – I don't take that lightly.

So you may say, "I am glad I am not a pastor or a teacher." Well, look at what Jesus said to not just pastors and teachers – but ALL of his followers:

*And I tell you this, you must give an account
on judgment day for every idle word
you speak.* (*Matthew 12:36*)

Jesus just got everybody's attention. Every teenager texting to friends; every post that you have put onto social media; every child talking to their parent; every parent who has lectured their children – every word. Jesus says that God will review every word at the end of your life when you meet Him face-to-face. Why? Because words are a big deal – they are powerful.

2. We have all made mistakes with our words.

James says it very clearly:

*Indeed, we all make many mistakes. For if we could
control our tongues, we would be perfect and could also
control ourselves in every other way.* (*James 3:2*)

Here is the reality: I've blown it, you've blown it, we've all blown it, all of us. If we could control our tongues, we would be perfect and could also control ourselves in every way.

You have, I have, every person reading this has made mistakes with their words. The reason we need this book is because ALL of us have messed up one relationship or another with words. We have chosen to go negative and not positive with what we say. And when we go negative, we mess up our relationships, causing them to go negative, too.

Now here's the great news: Welcome to Real Life – we've all made mistakes. God can forgive you. There's grace for you. And you're not reading this now to beat yourself up over what you wish you could take back. 'I wish I hadn't said that.' 'I wish I didn't post that.' 'I wish I hadn't emailed that.' But today, we can all hit 'reset' by grace, and allow Jesus and what He did on the cross to forgive us and give us a new beginning. Let's decide, "You know what? I'm going to start changing RIGHT NOW and I'm not going the way I've always gone with my words."

James offers the motivation to change our words by giving illustrations of just how powerful words can be – he gives some positive illustrations and a negative illustration as well.

Let's look at verses 3 and 4:

> *We can make a large horse go wherever*
> *we want by means of a small bit in its mouth.*
> *And a small rudder makes a huge ship turn*
> *wherever the pilot chooses to go, even though*
> *the winds are strong.* (James 3:3-4)

Words are like a small rudder on a boat.

In case you haven't seen a rudder lately – know that it is quite small compared to the whole boat. Usually you can't even see the rudder – but this tiny mechanism in the back of the boat tells this big ship where to go. James is illustrating to us that in the same way you can say something very small to someone that ends up changing the course of their life and moves them in God's direction. Your words turn the direction of your life by what you say. If you say, 'I'll never amount to anything' or 'I'll never get there' or 'This could never change,' you're literally turning your heart that way by what you just said. How about this instead? 'I'm not going to give up' and 'God's going to come through' and 'There's always hope' and 'God can move mountains' and 'I'm moving toward a dream that God's given me.' The words literally direct my heart. But watch this – it's not just you.

Did you know that your words can change your entire marriage? Your family? Every person around you? Just by what you say. Positive words can move you in one direction; negative words move you in another. Negative words move a family in one direction, positive words move a family in another.

But notice what else James says ...

> *In the same way, the tongue is a small thing*
> *that makes grand speeches. But a tiny spark*
> *can set a great forest on fire.* (James 3:5)

We can all relate to this. A small spark – a tiny match – can create major devastation. I might say something, and it seems like no big deal to me, but it ends up injuring not just one person – it affects many people and travels further than I ever thought. It damages lives I never imagined it could, and that one thing that I even forgot I said is like a smoldering spark sitting there. And that person's heart was dry ground and now it's a raging fire that has spread. What just happened? I said something. That's how powerful words are.

In the same way, one small word – 'Hey, I'm praying for you' or 'Hey, I just wanted you to know I'm thinking about you' or 'Hey, I just want you to know that God wants the best for you and He loves you.' I mean, think about it! That one word can change the direction for that person's life in the same way.

Last summer, my sons, my brother, and I went on our annual 'man trip'. We camped at 10,000 feet in the Sierra Nevada mountains. One night, while looking over three different mountain ranges, we were watching the sun go down. It was a beautiful and amazing moment! Then, as the sun was going down, and we kept looking at the skyline, it got really awkward because the sun had been going down for two hours by then! The entire ridgeline was still glowing. And finally, our guide said we weren't watching the sunset – we were watching a forest fire. One that we later found out was started by one person, with a small spark, and it was done intentionally. Over 100,000 acres were destroyed by one person's actions.

James says – here is your choice – how will you use your words? You can help guide people in a positive direction and direct them toward God and good, or you can go in a negative direction and cause a lot of damage and destruction.

This is how powerful words are and how important this is:

3. We all have a choice with our words.

In order for you to get the most out of this book, I want you to think about a significant relationship that you have. A relationship that you view as vital. This may be your spouse, your children, your parents, a best friend, or even a coworker. The message in this chapter – and for this entire book - is crucial to the health of that relationship. We all have a choice with our words, and you have control in consistently making the right choices.

We are 100% responsible for our words. You can't decide what somebody does to you. You can't decide where you were born. You can't decide maybe what schools you went to as a child. But what you are 100% responsible for is your words. You can't even choose what that person said to you! But guess what? You can choose what you say back to them. That's the reason why God is going to hold us accountable - because we are 100% responsible for them. It's a choice!

Counselor Gary Chapman said this about words: "Communication is basically an act of the will."[4]

You have to decide some things. In a minute, I want to share with you three decisions I make every day with my words and so do you.

By choosing to use my words differently, I can change the relationship.

> *Words kill, words give life;*
> *they are either poison or fruit – you choose.*
> (*Proverbs 18:21 MSG*)

Bookmark this page of the book. Highlight or underline "you choose." This is the main message. Really, the words that come out of our mouth are OUR responsibility. We're not FORCED to say them. It's

OUR choice. 'I'm going to kill their dream right now'; 'I'm going to kill their self-esteem right now' – or – 'I'm going to bring life to this situation' – and – 'I'm going to bring fruit to this.'

You actually get to choose the words that come out of your mouth. You have 100% responsibility for them, right? They're not forced on you. They are your choice, to bring life and value to the people and the relationships around you. That's what you were designed to do. And they were designed to run on those positive words.

Imagine with me for a minute. By your front door, or there in the foyer of your apartment or house, you have a big stack of $100 bills. A big, big stack. It's in the millions. It's right by your front door, right there. Let's say you walk out of that door every day and you just pass that stack of bills. When you go to school. When you go to work. You look at it. You get in your car. You back out of the driveway. You look in your front yard and you see bare ground and say to yourself,

"It'd sure be nice to have some grass and some flowers and do some landscaping. I wish I could afford it. I just can't afford it."

Then you drive down the street a little bit and you see

a new coffee shop you've wanted to try. You say,

"I'd love to get a latté right now. I'd love to have one of those muffins right now. But I just can't afford it."

You drive a little bit further and you see a car you have always wanted.

"Man, I want that car. It'd be great to drive that car, but I just can't afford it."

Now that's just a ridiculous illustration, isn't it? You've got a stack of money; go do something about it! Go change all the stuff you say you can't afford to do!

It's the same way with words. Think about what we do in our own lives. We have a wealth within our words that's waiting to be spent on those we value. We have a wealth within the words that we say that's just waiting to be deposited into the lives of other people.

Yet we walk through life as if we're verbally bankrupt. We go through life saying, "My husband will never change... My wife is getting worse... My children don't respond... My friends are in desperate need of help; they're hurting..." Yet we walk around like we are verbally bankrupt when we have a wealth within our words.

Words are powerful. They strengthen. They build. We

have the choice in how to use them. We can use them in fruitful ways or in poisonous ways. What would happen if you started to deposit into the people that you value? What if you started using your words and started investing in them? Instead of complaining about the people in your life and criticizing them, what if you started depositing words that will actually change the relationships in your life? And instead of acting like you're verbally bankrupt, what would happen if you realized that you have the most valuable thing in the world? Words are your most valuable possession.

I can bring life. I can bring fruit. I can either poison the things around me or I can literally make my relationships very, very fruitful. Choose to encourage. Choose to use your words in a fruitful way. Choose to bring wealth with your words into the relationships that you value.

I am going to ask you to make one of three decisions today – right now. All from James – you may check all of them – but I am going to ask you to focus on one you will work on this week:

Decision #1: Be POSITIVE with <u>how</u> you say things.

Have your parents ever said you are in trouble not for

what you said but *how* you said it?

This week, focus on how you are coming across – use your words wisely.

> **People can tame all kinds of animals, birds, reptiles, and fish, but no one can tame the tongue. It is restless and evil, full of deadly poison.** (*James 3:7*)

> **A gentle answer deflects anger, but harsh words make tempers flare.** (*Proverbs 15:1*)

Let's to decide today that we are going to work on how we say things – how we come across. We have to be careful how we say it. Because communication is a lot more than just the words we use.

One university study has shown that only 7% of communication is words. But 55% of communication is your body language![5] Over half of how you say something to someone is from your body language! Imagine your child has just asked you if you would take them to the swimming pool today. But you have to get all of your errands done before the BBQ you're hosting tonight, so there just isn't time today to enjoy a trip to the pool. What does your child look like right now? Sagged shoulders, crossed arms, furrowed brow, and a deep frown. No words are coming out of your child's mouth right now, but there is NO DOUBT the message she is conveying, right? Body language can sometimes say it all!

The *tone* of your voice accounts for 38% of how you communicate – specifically, *how* you say something.

Maybe you need to reign in your words. Tame *how* you say it.

Let's take a look at James 1 again, and let me show you this verse – this is a great verse that will help your family and your friendships. It's great to memorize. It's very simple, but very powerful.

> ***Understand this, my dear brothers and sisters:***
> ***You must all be quick to listen, slow to speak,***
> ***and slow to get angry.*** *(James 1:19)*

Some verses don't need a lot of explanation. What is James saying?

Decision #2: Be POSITIVE <u>when</u> you say it.

When you say something is just as important as *what* you actually say. For some of us, we need to work on hitting the pause button. Especially when we are angry. When anger is stirring up, don't say the first thing that comes to your mind! When you're really angry, don't even say the second thing that comes to your mind! Back up, hit pause.

We don't exactly live in a nation of listeners, do we? We live in a nation of talkers: 'Hear what I'm saying!' and if you can't hear it, 'I'm going to say it louder!' We struggle with listening; it's sort of built into our culture. Like, back in the day, when Will Rogers said this about our Congress: "Congress is so strange. A man gets up to speak and says nothing. Nobody listens. And then everybody disagrees."[6]

Does that sound like anyone you know? Listening just is not our natural preference. Most of us would rather be the ones speaking rather than the ones listening. You could really do yourself a big favor with words if you would just pause and listen before speaking. Choose to pause and take a step back and, by your actions, tell the other person, 'I'm going to listen to what you're saying instead of thinking about what I'm going to say next.'

Be quick to listen. Be slow to speak.
Most of us filter whatever we hear through our own opinions, through what we're going to say next. Some experts say that on average, we only hear 20% of what the other person says. Isn't that scary? People are trying to share their hearts, their opinions, their perspective, but we're only getting about 20% of that.

We have to change that.

We have to learn to use our ears.

We have to work on this.

> **Anyone who answers without listening is foolish and confused.** (*Proverbs 18:13 NCV*)

I would encourage you to take James 1:19 or Proverbs 18:13 and put it on your screen saver or on your refrigerator at home. Let's just get some verses that will change our relationships and write them on our hearts. Because we need to choose not just *how* we say something, but *when* we say it. We just need to push PAUSE. And step back. Before we speak. Maybe you need to choose this week to listen more and talk less.

Decision #3: Be POSITIVE <u>why</u> you say it.

At the beginning of the chapter of James 3, James tells us that we will give an account to God for what we say. Isn't that a sobering truth? But he takes the power of words to a whole other level – he is actually saying when you hurt people with your words, you are actually insulting God.

> **Sometimes your words praise our Lord and our father, and sometimes it curses those who have been made in the image of God.** (*James 3:9*)

God created every single person in His image. He created each person that you choose to insult. Before they were ever born, while they were still in their mother's womb, God put His fingerprints and His unique design on them. God has a plan for the person you are making fun of and He has a purpose for the person you are talking about. Now, you might say, 'well, they're not fulfilling their purpose because they said this and they did that.' Our judgment of how they fulfill their life's purpose is irrelevant.

Why we should say positive words is because the person we are speaking to is a child of God, just like us. Once we think about each person as who they truly are, a child made in the image of our God, how can we continue to speak badly either about them or to them? When you speak against God's own creation, you are actually insulting the God who made them for an incredible purpose. And for them to reach that purpose, someone has to begin speaking positive words into them.

But if you choose to insult other people, and to go negative with your words, it's actually an attack on the honor which God deserves. God hears every word that we say and we will all answer to Him for every word that we choose to say. We all have to come to a place where we decide – if God made everyone in His image, and He hears every word we utter, and I will answer to Him for them – then I will choose to honor Him with my words.

James continues:

> **And so blessing and cursing come pouring out of the same mouth. Surely, my brothers and sisters, this is not right!** (*James 3:10*)

We all have the same identity. We are all created in the same image of God and when I speak against you, I am speaking against the God who created all of us. And I need to remember that I am a child of God, so that I can be consistent with who I am by what I say.

> **Does a spring of water bubble out with both fresh water and bitter water? Does a fig tree produce olives, or a grapevine produce figs? No, and you can't draw fresh water from a salty spring.** (*James 3:11-12*)

I think he's trying to be funny here. He's trying to lighten the mood. Like, do you go out to the fig trees and say, 'Hey, I'm going to go grab some olives off the fig tree?' You don't do that. Or go to the grapevine for some figs? 'Hey, I'm going to grab some figs off of the grapevine.' It would be like me saying today, "Does a chicken lay coffee mugs? LOL." He is disarming us with humor.

James is giving the reason WHY you say positive words to other people. A fresh well can't produce salt water. You're a follower of Christ, you're a child of God, and if you are, decide NOW to honor God by what you say. This is all next-level stuff! And what he is saying here is, when you speak, the reasons why you're saying whatever you're saying is because you either know who you are, or you've forgotten who you are. The reason you are saying that is because you know that they are a child of God or you've forgotten that they are God's creation. James is saying to remember who you are. In other words, before you evaluate your words, evaluate your self-worth.

Have you heard the phrase: 'Hurt people hurt people'? That is absolutely true. When you hurt, you have a low self-esteem. You're trying to defend yourself. You're trying to make sure you're heard. You're trying to make sure you stand up for yourself, so everybody knows that you're awesome, you're popular, you're great. You have to hurt someone else so they don't see how much you are hurting.

But when you know who you are in Christ, and your identity is settled in Him, then you can just bless –

even your enemies – even people who speak against you. Because you know that they are created in the image of God and you know who you are is not based on anything that they are saying. And all of a sudden what happens is your identity is secure in who you are in Christ and therefore you don't have to curse with your words or go negative towards someone else. This is a life-changing idea.

The big question is: Where is your identity right now? Is your identity in who you are in Christ? Or something else? You can figure it out by the words you use.

People who have a low self-esteem and who are insecure, those are the people who are saying negative things. They are. I hope that your identity is not built on anything that you can lose. I hope your identity is not in your job, because you can lose your job. If you try to build your identity on how good looking you are, one day you are going to look in the mirror and realize those good looks are gone! Welcome to Real Life. You can build your life on being popular – you're not always going to be popular.

However, you can't lose your identity in Christ. You will always be a son or daughter of the King of the Universe who is priceless and worth the sacrifice of God's Son on the cross.

If you build your identity on anything that can be taken away from you, you're going to be insecure, and insecurity is at the root of your hurtful words. But, when your identity is in who you are in Christ, and in who He designed you to be, then you value yourself. Your security is in Him, and then you can bring value to others by what you say. Because you reflect Jesus, and you are created in the image of Jesus, you are going to be able to bless with your words.

Let me give you a prayer that I hope you'll pray every day. I pray this prayer every time before I get on stage. I know I blow it. I know I do. And I have. And I need to choose each of these decisions at one time or another in my life. But I pray this prayer because I take very seriously what I say, and I would ask you to pray the prayer yourself every day:

> *May the words of my mouth and the meditation of my heart be pleasing to you, O Lord, my Rock and my Redeemer.* (Psalm 19:14)

This prayer will move your words toward positive and away from negative. Every time. Prayer connects your heart to God's heart, and God's heart is always to bless. If you decide to please GOD with everything you say, you decided that words honor Him and others. This respect for God and others moves your words away from hurtful and toward healing. Because I want my words to please God, I don't care if my words please someone else. I don't care if they get 18 likes or 18,000 likes on social media. "Lord, I want my words to please You. You're my Lord, my Rock! You're my Redeemer!"

Pray this every day and watch your words and your relationships transform.

Decide what you are going to work on this week: *how* you say it – in the relationships that you say you value. *When* you say it – maybe you hit pause and really think about it – and make sure anger doesn't have a foothold.

Why you say it – I am a child of God – I get to bless, because God has blessed me.

Maybe you don't know where to start. You can choose one decision, but you're in this cycle, and you don't know how to break the cycle. Maybe you're in a cycle of negative words from your parents, and it's been passed down for generations. "This is just how my parents talked and I can't change that!" No! You *can* change that. It can be simply deciding to stop using negative words. And you're going to stop that cycle. And you're going to create a generation of blessing with words.

I heard a story recently. There is an old man jogging

slowly on a high school track. The football players are working out on the field in the middle, doing wind sprints while he was jogging. He thought, "As long as those kids are doing wind sprints, I think I can jog." So he keeps jogging and they keep doing wind sprints. Jogging – wind sprints. Jogging – wind sprints. He jogs two more miles than he's ever jogged in his life, and finally, he had to quit. He stopped. And when he stopped, all of the young football players collapsed. Then one of the young football players crawled over to him and said, "Man, I am so glad you stopped jogging because our coach said as long as that old man keeps running around the track, you guys can keep doing wind sprints!"

Some of you are thinking:

"I want my marriage to change. And if they would just start talking nice, then I will start talking nice."

or

"If my kids are just respectful, I'll be honoring to them!"

or

"If that person in my work place will stop being negative, then I'm going to be positive!"

But no! You stop the cycle right now! You stop. And you back up. And say, "I am going to be positive with my words."

This week, my words will please God and bless people.

We're going to stop the cycle. NO more hurtful words.

We're going to stop the cycle. NO more negative posts.

We're going to stop the cycle. NO more hurtful tweets.

We're going to stop the cycle. NO more mean texts.

And today we are going to decide that our words will please God, and they will bless other people.

PRAYER:
> **May the words of my mouth and the meditation**
> **of my heart be pleasing to you, O Lord, my**
> **Rock and my Redeemer.** *(Psalm 19:14)*

Chapter Footnotes:
[1]*The 7 Biggest Complaints Of Long-Married Couples (Sara Schwartz, Grandparents.com)*
[2]*The Top Things Every Woman (and Her Husband) Should Know*
(dmagazine.com/publications/d-magazine/2010/may/divorce-in-dallas/)
[3]*fatherhood.org/fatherhood/the-affects-of-an-emotionally-unavailable-dad*
[4]*The Marriage You've Always Wanted, by Gary Chapman, Moody Publishers, Chicago, 2009*
[5]*Is Nonverbal Communication a Numbers Game?, Psychology Today,*
Blog entry by Jeff Thompson, Ph.D., Oct. 6, 2016
[6]*willrogerstoday.com/will_rogers_quotes*

"

*A cheerful look brings joy
to the heart; good news makes
for good health.*

"

(Proverbs 15:30 NLT)

2

FOREST FIRE

Words spread like wildfire. Whether they are good or bad - the Gospel of Jesus or gossip about people – the words we share move beyond us rapidly once we say them. This chapter will unpack Gospel and gossip. We will discover together just how amazing and awesome it is when we speak Gospel, and just how dangerous and destructive it is when we gossip.

First, let's tackle the dangers of gossip. Do you know that we kind of dress up gossip? If I share it like a prayer request and maybe say it with a smile, gossip must be okay, right? And we don't think about it as much as other things that are also as dangerous. Take scissors, for example. Scissors can be nice. I've even seen scissors all decorated with polka dots and glitter.

I can even take a pair of scissors, get a red sheet of paper, fold it over once, cut it and make a nice paper heart. You can encourage someone else with the work of scissors and say, "I love you," right? But you also can take the scissors and cause a lot of damage. That's just how words are.

We've got to choose Gospel over gossip, but the first step is to realize just how dangerous gossip is, and just how hard the choice is to go Gospel instead of gossip. If we aren't careful, we dress up gossip really nice and it gets in our lives and we don't even know it's there. And running with gossip is a lot more dangerous than running with scissors.

I want to start out by looking at a couple of verses in the Bible that may seem irrelevant to this topic, but they have everything to do with it. This is a sad story, but it is real life.

That is what I love about the Bible – it is real. Real people. Real events. The Bible tells us what really happened. Fantasy novels or make-believe stories usually sugarcoat the heroes. Any rough edges or wrong turns are smoothed over. In make-believe stories, it seems like the hero always wins! Nothing bad ever happens to them. This is just another reason why I believe the Bible is true – it tells us what actually happened, not just what we wish had happened.

Let's see what really happened to a guy named John the Baptist.

a popular figure, to be sure, John the Baptist was the guy who was the last Old Testament prophet. He prepared the way for Jesus' ministry. He is the one who said *"Behold, the Lamb of God, who takes away the sin of the world!"* He baptized Jesus. Jesus started his ministry with John the Baptist. Jesus came up out of the water, and heaven opened, and a dove descended. And the heavenly Father said, *"This is my beloved Son, with whom I am well pleased."*

Don't you know that John the Baptist's baptism numbers went up after that?! John the Baptist knew he was there to point people to Jesus. Once Jesus came on the scene, John the Baptist said "I must decrease – He must increase." Truly a great attitude for our lives. I must decrease, and Jesus must increase! John the Baptist was a spiritual hero.

However, John the Baptist was also a fiery guy. He wore this rough camel skin and his preaching was as rough as his clothing. He spoke truth, but it was in-your-face, tell-you-what-you-needed-to-hear, not

what-you-wanted-to-hear truth. And one day, he went
off on the political leader of the time, King Herod.
He basically called him out in a sermon. He said that
King Herod was wrong and he should be doing a list
of things that he was not doing. One of the things that
John called King Herod out on was his wife. John said
that King Herod should not have even married his
wife. A lot of consequences came from this, but this is
what happened:

> *For Herod had arrested and imprisoned*
> *John as a favor to his wife Herodias (the former*
> *wife of Herod's brother Philip). John had*
> *been telling Herod, "It is against God's*
> *law for you to marry her."*
> (Matthew 14:3-4)

The circumstances read like a modern day soap opera:
Herodias, King Herod's wife, was formerly married to
his brother, Philip. When Philip and Herodias were
married, they attended a family reunion at King Herod's
palace. King Herod saw Herodias and decided that he
didn't like his own wife anymore; he liked Philip's wife.
He didn't care that Philip was his brother and Herodias
was his brother's wife! He convinced Herodias to
divorce Philip, and Herod also divorced his own wife.
Then King Herod and Herodias got married. Can you

imagine the family get togethers after this?! Awkward!

John the Baptist spoke out against all this and said – no! He reminded Herod and those who listened to his sermons that God takes marriage seriously and all this wife-swapping and pleasure-seeking is wrong! You are not doing what God wants you to do. John called out King Herod and Herodias! Of course, this was true, but Herodias was mad.

Did you know that when people are doing the wrong thing, they don't like you telling them they are doing the wrong thing? It's called pride. Herodias is upset – she doesn't like being on John the Baptist's Twitter feed; she doesn't like getting called out.

It kind of shows you how powerful a wife's role can be in the home – 'Honey, could you get some milk on the way home, and can you also arrest John the Baptist?' Herod agrees and Herodias' words would eventually trick Herod into killing him. But you may ask, what does this have to do with gossip?

Every day we choose to invest our words in gossip or Gospel.

The gossip in Jesus' day about John the Baptist spread everywhere.

The word on the street was that John has been arrested.

Jesus is our example – let me show you what he does right after this happens to John . . .

> **After John was arrested, Jesus went to Galilee and <u>told the good news that comes from God</u>.**
> *(Mark 1:14 CEV)*

The people were seeing that John the Baptist had been arrested and they were thinking, 'This is bad' – people were saying that John the Baptist shouldn't have said that; and that he had a great ministry, but he just made a bad choice. They thought, if he wouldn't have called out Herod's wife on Twitter, then he could continue his ministry! But Jesus didn't choose to gossip! He chose to continue to share the Gospel! We see that after John was arrested, Jesus didn't spread gossip, he spread the Gospel.

Gospel literally means good news! And Gospel is for ALL of us. Very simply, John 3:16 says "For God so loved the world that He gave His one and only Son, that whoever believes in Him shall not perish but have eternal life." The Gospel is that Jesus came, and He died, and was buried. And He rose again. He wants to live in your heart. He can forgive you. Turn from your way and follow God's way. He can give you the hope of heaven. It's the Gospel. It's good news!

But the Gospel is not only for saving people. We need Gospel everyday! We all need good news every day! We are designed to run on the love of God and the Good News about Him. And we are designed to run on and focus on the good things that God is doing in us and around us. But there is a choice, we must choose that our lives be about Gospel; how we smile, how we share, what we say – Gospel.

We can choose to share Gospel everyday – or – our lives can be about gossip.

Don't miss this. I'll say it one more time – even if the news is true! Some of us think we are off the hook, because the news we are sharing is true! We think it is not gossip if we are shaing the facts. But it is bad news whether or not it's true! Fact: John the Baptist was arrested. Fact: Herodias was not at all happy. Fact: King Herod was doing a favor because his wife runs the house.

But Jesus says, you know what? I'm not going to share bad news, I am going to continue to share good news. And that is what your life should be about as well. What you should say should be good news about God and what He is doing.

What would happen if you focused on the Gospel, not gossip?

Every person needs GOSPEL. Nobody needs gossip.

Everyday, we make the choice. Gospel? or gossip?

ESPN SportsCenter is a great example of how gossip works. Monday is the best time to watch ESPN SportsCenter, because that's the day they review all the football games from the weekend, right? And that's when guys wearing really nice suits, sitting behind really nice desks, who get paid a lot of money, tell you what *should* have happened instead of what did, right? And so, they rewind the plays and say: the coach should have called a timeout ... the quarterback should have thrown it to the tight-end – he was wide-open! ... I can't believe they didn't go for the two point conversion there ... That coach is a moron!" It is called Monday morning quarterbacking. ESPN is an innocent and fun analysis of an American sport. However, gossip is not innocent or fun for those being talked about.

We are great at Monday-morning-quarterbacking everybody else's decisions – just not our own.

Do you know what gossip is? It's like Monday-morning-quarterbacking everybody else's life. Guess what that does? It keeps the focus off of what God is doing in our life, how much He loves us, and how He wants to use us to share Gospel. We can't share the Gospel because we get tied up in the gossip.

Now take a minute to circle this word or write it down somewhere: Gospel.

Gospel is the option to choose instead of gossip. Remember you can choose:

> *Words kill, words give life;*
> *they are either poison or fruit – you choose.*
> *(Proverbs 18:21 MSG)*

You choose. Gospel gives life; it gives love; it gives hope.

Or gossip, which is damaging, degrading, killing people's reputation, poisoning how people see them.

> *A gossip goes around telling secrets,*
> *but those who are trustworthy*
> *can keep a confidence.*
> *(Proverbs 11:13)*

Gossip is everywhere:
- Television – celebrity shows like Talk Soup, Entertainment Tonight, Extra, even the news
- Magazines – scandals and spin
- Facebook, Twitter, Instagram, even Snapchat

- It happens in the office, on the phone or at the weekend party

We need to get away from gossip. There are three main reasons, because it causes three specific things that are not good.

GOSSIP CAUSES GUILT

After you gossip – do feel better about life? No, not long term.

Let's be honest. It makes us feel good for a second, right? Maybe we feel better for a few days because we got to vent with a few people ... got even. We use the excuse that we needed to get it off our chest, so it's for our own good to tell this to someone else. It may feel good for a moment. But it isn't satisfying; it leaves us feeling empty. It zaps our strength. We feel guilty and we can't fix what happened. We find ourselves saying, "Why did I say that?" And suddenly, we realize why God wants us to stay away from it.

> *Their lives became full of every
> kind of wickedness, sin, greed, hate,
> envy, murder, quarreling, deception,
> malicious behavior, and gossip.*
> (*Romans 1:29*)

Do you notice that gossip is on the same list as murder?

I don't have a gun in my bag; I don't have a grenade. I'm not going to kill anybody. But words can kill people by killing their reputation; killing their dreams; killing their character; destroying things around them; mess up all kinds of things. And we think that it's not a big deal. But it causes guilt, just like you took somebody out and buried him in the backyard. It is overwhelming to look back and say, 'I can't believe I did that.' And we try to make it look nice. We put glitter on it or we put some polka dots on gossip and we think if we do it a certain way it's not really gossip.

Here are some different kinds of gossipers.

Prayer Request Gossipers: "We really need to pray for Susie; she is trying to quit smoking and I saw her on her lunch break smoking two at a time."

Do you know a Prayer Request Gossiper? We think if we wrap it in a prayer request, then it's no longer gossip!

Bless-Their-Heart Gossipers: "Did you hear who she went out with? Wasn't she dating someone else last week? Did you see her outfit? Her hair just isn't working. I love her though - bless her heart."

Do you know a Bless-Their-Heart Gossiper? We think if we tag a 'bless their heart' at the end, we're off the hook for gossiping.

Don't Know When to be Quiet Gossipers: On the phone, on text; 'Their marriage is struggling. My neighbors have problems.' Talk and talk and talk.

Do you know any of these?

Just Tell the Truth/Macho Gossipers: "If they didn't want anybody to know, they shouldn't have said anything to me! ... I would tell them to their face, but since they're not here, I will just tell you instead."

Know any of these?

And you may be saying, 'Well, I'm off the hook. I don't do any of these things!" You say that you don't gossip, and you don't repeat rumors, or talk badly about people?

> **Wrongdoers eagerly listen to gossip; liars pay close attention to slander.** *(Proverbs 17:4)*

Did you know it's wrong just to listen to it? Why so serious? Why should we not even listen to it? Not even entertain it? Because:

GOSSIP CAUSES PAIN

There's pain involved with gossip and all of us have experienced it. When it happens, we can't fix the pain that it's caused. God can heal and God can forgive, but it is hard to fix this power of gossip and the pain it causes. It's like the story I heard of a rural pastor out in West Texas. He lived in a small town and rumors started swirling about this guy out of nowhere. Months went by and the rumors got more and more fabricated, more and more ridiculous, and also more and more hurtful about him and his family. Finally, a guy came to his door at the back of the parsonage and this guy stood on the porch and says, "Pastor, I'm the one who started all the gossip, and I just want you to forgive me. I'm really sorry."

And without saying a word, the pastor went back into the house and came out with a feather pillow. He cut it open and he let those feathers fly in the West Texas wind. I mean those feathers started going everywhere – in the gutters, in the mailbox, all over the fields and the animals. And this guy's watching all the feathers fly everywhere in every direction. And after the whole pillowcase is empty, the pastor says, "Listen, I forgive you. But to fix the gossip, you'd have to go find every one of those feathers, and there's no way you can do that. But I do forgive you."

He was saying forgiveness can happen in a moment. But gossip is so powerful that once it's let loose, it literally goes everywhere, immediately compounding, and causing all of this pain that we can't even imagine. And it is impossible to fix the damage you have caused. And we have all been damaged by it.

> ***They visit me as if they were my friends, but all the while they gather gossip, and when they leave, they spread it everywhere.***
> *(Psalm 41:6)*

Here is another illustration. Two guys meet during the day, just having lunch or coffee. "So did you hear about Rob? Man, he is struggling with [fill in the blank] ... Man, I think his marriage is ending ... Did you hear about what one of his kids is dealing with? ... And don't get me started about what one of his coworkers said."

Then those guys look at each other – and say, "Poor Rob." And then they walk away and have just left Rob's reputation lying there on the ground. See?

We have all been damaged by the words that people have said about us. And all of us, if we are honest, have hurt other people with our words in some way.

Maybe you shared something with a Christian, and a few days later, it's everywhere.

Maybe you have been hurt by gossip.

Maybe you are the one who spread the gossip.

Maybe you are the one who talks too much; you are not intentional about it, but slowly you are chipping away.

Maybe you are the one at the office saying, "Can you believe he got a promotion? He can never finish a project without my help, why does he deserve that position?"

Each day, we are bombarded with hundreds of thousands of them. Words have the power to build up or break down. They can uplift and enlighten or depress and destroy. We all have control over the words we use and we must learn to choose them carefully.

GOSSIP CAUSES SEPARATION

Have you ever known some people who were really close, but then something was said, something else was said; a few careless words, and all of a sudden you look up and not only are they not friends, but they have become enemies! Gossip will do that.

Do you see how gossip causes separation? This is why we have to stay away from it, because God's plan is harmony and connection, and the enemy's plan is disharmony, disunity and separation.

> *A troublemaker plants seeds of strife;*
> *gossip separates the best of friends.*
>
> (*Proverbs 16:28*)

Who are the people who you have hurt by your words, by your gossip? What relationships have ended? Maybe you have friendships that were really, really strong at one point, and aren't quite the same anymore. Maybe it was with a family member and now that relationship is broken. Maybe you've destroyed someone's character or hurt their feelings. And the list goes on and on and on. For some of you, maybe you were the one who was burned by someone else's words.

I want you to know that God loves you so much. He knows how fragile your heart is and He cares about you. He deeply wants to take His healing ointment and just drop it into your wounds and bring healing to your life.

God's plan is to bring us together – to bring connection. The enemy's plan is to tear us apart – to cause disunity. We need to offer forgiveness. And we need to ask for it as well. 'God, forgive us for the times we have not thought about how powerful words are, and how dangerous and destructive gossip is.' We had these glittery scissors in our bag and we used them for hurt and not for good. We need to get this out of our lives. Ask God to bring healing where we have been hurt and maimed by this path of destruction called gossip.

The question we need to ask is:

How do we move on from here? We know that the tongue can leave a path of destruction. We know that gossip hurts and maims. How do we change things? How do we raise the bar spiritually? How do we say, "Okay, I am not going to live my life like that anymore," and, "I want to move forward and I want to change the way I live life." How do you begin to do that? How do you overcome gossip?

You can't wrestle with gossip and win – but you can replace it.

Very simply: Stop talking ABOUT people and start talking TO people. This is what we need to do. It's a lot different to talk to someone's face than to talk about someone behind their back. And, in love, to say the truth, but to say 'you're the one that is hearing this.' Today, let's decide: I'm not going to spread gossip anymore. I'm going to spread Gospel. I'm going to share good news. My mouth is going to help people to focus on God; His love, His plan, His purpose for them and this world.

John was Jesus' cousin and biggest fan; he was put in prison because he spoke out against a politician who was making immoral choices. He was wrongfully and unfairly put in prison. What did Jesus do? He didn't go about spreading gossip – He went about spreading the Gospel. Jesus displayed how to make the choice.

What if you're not a Christian yet? In other words, the example of Jesus isn't enough of a motivation? Why would you want to spread Gospel? Here's why:

GOSPEL STRENGTHENS PHYSICAL HEALTH

Research done at the University of Arizona demonstrated that the words used by parents, in talking to their children, directly affected the health of their children for decades. This research was part of the Harvard Stress Study[7], a 35-year study which followed many parameters of stress and health in the family. It's proven that what you say to your kids either makes them healthier, or in reverse, what you say makes them more sick!

In this study, it was found that, regardless of other health risk factors, children from loving parents who often used positive words and regularly talked about good news had less coronary artery disease, less high blood pressure, fewer stomach ulcers, and were less likely to become alcoholics than those kids from parents who were consistently negative and talking about bad things or saying bad things to them.

This research discovered what the Bible already tells us:

> *A cheerful look brings joy to the heart,*
> *and good news gives health to the bones.*
> *(Proverbs 15:30)*

Gospel is part of the New Complete Breakfast!

This is really amazing information. This is like a brand-new part of a complete breakfast commercial, right? What makes a complete breakfast? Cereal, four slices of toast, a gallon of orange juice, three eggs and a protein bar? What if the best thing for your kid's health is to start each morning by talking nicely to them – to share positive talk? To talk about the Good News – to speak to them about God and His plan for them. I have a great new revolutionary health program: speak good news. As parents, we can get so busy with life and while we make sure our kids have a complete breakfast – we forget their greatest need – for us to share the Good News with them. We need to speak positive words over them and into their lives! When we speak Gospel to them, we will strengthen them and provide the building blocks for a strong and healthy future. We should choose Gospel because it brings good health to everyone around us. Alternatively, gossip will destroy our health and the health of those around us.

GOSPEL PROVIDES EMOTIONAL HEALING

We don't talk about it, but there is an emotional drain that gossip brings into our lives, not only when we share it, but also when we listen to it; when we are victims of it, and also when we are part of it. It can emotionally drain us! However, Gospel can provide emotional healing.

Here are two practical things that you can do this week that will help you commit to Gospel.

First: Read the Gospel. I encourage you to read the Bible every day. You can even get a free Bible app on your phone. Start with the book of James or even the book of Proverbs. Just read a chapter a day. Commit. Decide, 'I need Truth in my life. I need Gospel in my heart so that I can share Gospel.' And just read the Bible. **Before you get on Facebook, face The Book.** Yes, that just happened.

Read the Bible. Say, 'I'm going to get the Good News in my life before I turn on the bad news. I'm going to get this on my heart before I get on Facebook and see that everyone else is complaining about or posting negatively about someone without mentioning their names – we've all seen that, right? Have you ever thought that was about you? Well, now you can start your day by getting into God's Word.

Good News = The Bible

Good News = God's Word

Now you can turn the other cheek, and instead of getting back at someone who hurts you with gossip, you can choose to share Gospel. When you start your day in God's Word and have His healing words written on your heart, you no longer feel the need to perpetuate negativity. Instead, you stop the cycle of gossip and we start spreading the Good News.

Second: Pray out loud with the people that you love. Don't be the person who only prays silently in their head. Silent prayer is awesome and God loves any prayer. But the power of spoken prayer, shared with a loved one, is a powerful next step.

Married couples: Pray out loud with your spouse. Try it one time this week. Hold hands when you're doing it and just say, "God, thank you for my spouse. Bless them. May your will be done in their heart. And God, thank you for the relationship we have, and help us to grow toward you."

An amazing benefit of praying with your spouse: you cannot stay mad at someone with whom you are praying.

Parents: Pray over your kids out loud before they go to sleep. Make sure the last thing they hear is not 'Did you do your homework? Okay, goodnight!' and close the door. No! Go by their bed, kneel down next to them, and say, "God, thank you for my child. Bless them. I love them and I thank you that you love them, too. You have a plan - a purpose - that is beyond anything they can possibly imagine. You're going to do great things through them. May they believe it and may you bless them for it."

Pray with your friends: Pray over your friends. You should get together with them, and pray out loud. "God, thank you for our friendship. We ask for your protection over us. We ask that you help us to continue to build each other up and help us to inspire one another to stay close with you, Lord."

When we pray the Gospel out loud, it will heal them and it will heal us. It may take time, but it will heal. Gospel is emotionally healing.

> *Like cold water to a weary soul,*
> *so is good news from a distant land.*
> (*Proverbs 25:25 NASB*)

You are more tired than you think, emotionally. And

the way you rejuvenate emotionally and spiritually is you get God's Word in your heart and you pray with others. Gospel is 'like cold water to a weary soul' and will spiritually renew your soul.

GOSPEL IGNITES SPIRITUAL RENEWAL
It ignites you from the inside out! That's why the enemy wants you to stay away from Gospel. And just hang out with gossip. We don't realize we need Gospel and the renewal it provides, but when we are in such a negative world where we are watching bad news, hanging out with people who share bad news, live in a Monday morning quarterback mentality, it drains us. This negative world leaves us empty. But Jesus gives us the example; Jesus spread the good news. When He did, people changed. You can't wrestle with gossip. You can only beat gossip by replacing it with Gospel.

When the true message, the Good News,
first came to you, you heard about the hope it
offers. So your <u>faith</u> and <u>love</u> are based on what
you <u>hope</u> for, which is kept safe for you in heaven.
(Colossians 1:5 GN)

You need one of the three things that Gospel brings:

FAITH: Maybe you have not yet placed your faith in God. You haven't received Jesus as your personal Lord and Savior. You know about Him, and you're 'religious', but do you have a relationship with Him today? Place your faith in God who sent his Son, who died on a cross, who rose again, and wants to live in your heart. Faith, that nothing in this world can move, is what you can have today.

LOVE: We live in a world that sings about love, that has whole radio stations and music streams committed to love songs, but doesn't really know what love is. This is how we know what love is: Jesus Christ laid down His life for us, and this is how they'll know that we are His disciples, if we love each other. I'm going to encourage you to say 'I love you' a lot more often to the people you actually love.

If you're married, say 'I love you' before you leave for the day or before you get off the phone with that person. Every time. Don't be the husband who says, "I told her that I loved her on the day we got married. And if that changes, I'll let her know." Say 'I love you' when they leave and again, 'I love you,' when they come home each day. Tell your kids that you love them. Tell your parents that you love them. Tell your friends that you love them and share that love by just expressing it. Because we all need it in a world that is very cynical and full of gossip. And people who love each other hold each other in confidence and share Gospel.

HOPE: We all need hope! You may be facing a mountain right now; that mountain may seem impossible. It may feel like it's not going anywhere. Listen: God moves mountains and He can move that mountain in your life. There's always hope! Maybe you're going through a deep valley. He can deliver you from it or He can walk you all the way through it. Gospel strengthens our faith. Gospel shares love; Gospel brings hope; and that's what we all need. That's why we want to share that Good News – Gospel, not gossip.

Real Life is about the power of God's love at work in people's lives. Choose Gospel!

There is hope! What can we do? We can start the clean-up process. And it starts with our hearts.

Right after John the Baptist got arrested, from that time Jesus began to preach, saying,

> *"Change your hearts and lives,*
> *because the kingdom of heaven is near."*
> (*Matthew 4:17 NCV*)

I am going to encourage you to make a decision. Decide to ask Jesus to change your heart today. Choose: I am not going to have anything to do with gossip anymore. I'm not going to share it. I'm not going to listen to it. I'm going to be about Gospel. I'm going to be about the Good News. I'm going to strengthen people's faith. I'm going to share the love of God. And I'm going to bring hope to people's lives. And I'm going to let them love and help minister to me as well. It is Gospel over gossip.

But be careful, because gossip is everywhere. And it is powerful. And that is why the devil wants you to do it; because it can overwhelm the Gospel and the Good News that's all around us.

One week, as I was writing this, I was out jogging in my neighborhood, thinking about Gospel vs. gossip. I had it in my heart, and I decided to share Gospel wherever I go, no matter what. I'm jogging around the neighborhood, feeling good, when I saw a garbage truck coming down the street. Great, what better time to share Gospel than on garbage day? I was going to share some Gospel – smile and wave; I'm so thankful for somebody doing that job. As they drove by, I smiled and waved. And as that truck blew by me, I began to capture a whiff of wind – the stench coming off of that truck – it hit me. When was the last time you were next to a garbage truck? I forgot just how bad they smell! It was like a wall of odor – and it surrounded me! I had to stop running – I was not smiling – I was overwhelmed by it. I mean, I was just jogging, making great time, and suddenly I just stopped – the stench - I could not breathe. I was choked out! I literally went down to my knees, and thought, 'oh my word!' It was overwhelming and horrible and it didn't just smell, it stunk! I couldn't move! I waited and then I did the test smell thing. You know, daringly took a small sniff to see if it was still lingering. Yep! It's still there! And nope, I still can't breathe, and I can't move!

When this happened to me, I realized that this is why – listen – this is why the devil wants you to keep gossiping and to keep you away from the Gospel, because when you commit to Gospel, you live in a world that's got a wave of gossip ready for you. And gossip, if we're not careful, overwhelms Gospel, where people can't even see the Good News. They can't even sense God's love. They can't even know there's hope there. They can't even strengthen in their faith because gossip just comes by and it has the power to grind you to a screeching halt.

I want you to make a commitment this week: decide NOT to be a garbage truck. When you 'drive' through your family. When you 'drive 'through your office this week. When you 'drive' through your Facebook and social media accounts. Make this commitment: I am going to share Gospel.

You are going to have to get very serious about this.

This week, go out of your way to spread Good News. If you put your kids to bed without praying for them, go back in and wake them up and pray with them and bless them. If you forget to say I love you, call them back and say 'I love you.' You're going to help people. You're going to go out of your way this week. Instead of being a garbage truck with a huge wave of stench called gossip, you're going to bring beautiful news about the love of God and the good things He does, and the good things He's doing in your life.
Because He is always working!

This week:

I will choose Gospel over gossip.

I will go out of my way to spread Good News with my words.

PRAYER:
Lord, please forgive me for all of the times I have chosen gossip over Gospel. Today, I choose to move forward and fill my life with Gospel. From this day forward, no more sharing bad news. God, today, heal me and cleanse me. From the hurt I have caused, and from the hurt that I have

experienced through this. And God, this is a new day and I pray Gospel over my heart. I pray for mercy and grace over my heart. I pray for faith to be restored. Faith in what you can do through me. God, I pray that I connect closer with how real you are and closer to your love. I come back to your love, Lord, and I pray that you will give me courage to share Your love with everyone in my life. Even the people in my life that are unloveable right now. God, help me to love them. May Your love be expressed in everything that I do. And may I bring hope to those around me. You are good, Lord. Help me to share Good News. Amen.

Chapter Footnotes:
[7]From Best Practices to Breakthrough Impacts, May 2016, Center on the Developing Child at Harvard University, page 10

"

*An anxious heart
weighs a man down, but a
kind word cheers him up.*

"

(Proverbs 12:25)

3

THE SECRET KILLER

W e've been learning the power of words, right? Words have the power to lift up and strengthen both ourselves and others. And words have the power to tear down and weaken those around us. Well, just how much power do we have? Let's start with the guys. Did you know the average man uses 15,000 words a day? Now that's a lot of weapons. Fifteen thousand opportunities to apply this message to your life. Can you guess how many words the average woman uses a day? Are you sitting down? It's 30,000!

Ladies, this is why when you ask your husband a question at the end of the day, and he goes, "Huh ...," he is simply out of words – he's not being grumpy. He is at 15,001 and he has to wait until tomorrow to answer you. And ladies, this means you have twice as many opportunities as guys do to apply this message to your life. But guys, this also means we have to make every word count.

The most powerful thing that you have at your disposal in your life is *your words.*

The most powerful change agent that you have in the world to change relationships is *words.*

Words have destroyed more friendships than any other force. Words have killed more relationships than any other weapon. More dreams have been stopped, more hopes have been dashed, more self-worth has crumbled with the weapon of words than any other destructive tool.

The most powerful weapon in the world is words.

Words can be a powerful tool to bring life and vision, but they also carry more power than we realize to destroy and kill.

Every day you can choose one of two paths with your words. Compliments – encouraging people, speaking words of life; or complaints – which is like a poison that turns relationships toxic quickly and quietly.

Complaints are a secret killer.

If we are honest, we all tend to often lean towards complaining, don't we? We tend to get into this rhythm, or rut, of complaining about everything.

I want to show you one verse from the book of Philippians. The Apostle Paul wrote this next verse in his letter to the people of Philippi. The letter, we call the book of Philippians, is about joy. It's about being content. It's teaching us to say, 'whatever my circumstances are, God is good, and it's going to be okay, and I'm going to make the best of it.' And you may say, 'that's easy for Paul to say. He's probably on the beach somewhere writing this.' No, Paul wrote this letter from prison. People are controlling his schedule, people are controlling his time. He's not doing what he wants to do and he's not where he wants to be, but he makes this statement. This is a choice for all of us. And if you are a parent, this is a great verse to teach your kids:

> ***Do everything without complaining***
> ***and arguing.*** *(Philippians 2:14)*

Parents, you're welcome! Warning: if you teach this verse to your kids, you actually have to do it, too!

Paul wrote this while he had a lot to complain about,

yet he chose not to. Let me make you a promise: every day, every hour, every minute of your life, you can find something to complain about. But the Scripture tells us to do what Paul is doing here. He chooses to compliment. He's choosing to encourage the Philippians, to speak words of life. Why? Because complaining is like a poison that really can ruin our lives and everything else. The fact is that it is easy to slip into a mode of finding the negative things in life, and complaining about them, rather than finding the good things and complimenting those. We can easily go negative. We can start to find things to complain about instead of looking for the good things that God is doing.

It is easy to complain. It's like the story I heard recently of a guy who felt called to live as a monk for the rest of his life. He went to a monastery where he took a vow of silence, and he couldn't' speak for seven years. Then every seven years, he would come before the elders where he could only speak two words that best described what he had learned in those seven years of silence.

After the first seven years of silence, he stood before the elders and they asked him, "What do you have to say about what you've learned?"

"BAD FOOD."

(after seven more years of silence)

"HARD BED."

(seven years of more silence)

"I QUIT."

The elders then replied, "You might as well quit – you have done nothing but complain since you got here."

Complaints are easy to come up with – but God has a better plan: compliments. An appropriate word at an appropriate time. Compliments bring life. Complaints kill everything around them. Paul could have complained. Philippians chapter one could have started with, "bad food!" He is in prison! He could have easily said, "hard bed!" or probably more truth, "no bed!" He could have written, "This is horrible! I am a pastor and I am struggling, and this is so hard, and my life is so bad!" But he didn't do that. He is teaching us through this letter that we have a choice.

We can't choose our circumstances, but we can choose our words. He is teaching us that compliments bring life. He shows us that it is our choice to do everything without complaining. He didn't choose where he was; he couldn't choose what he did during the day, he couldn't choose his schedule, his food, or his bed. But he could choose his words. And so can we. We have a choice.

Our theme verse for this book, Proverbs 18:21, reminds us how powerful words are.

> *Words kill, words give life;*
> *they are either poison or fruit – you choose.*
> (*Proverbs 18:21 MSG*)

Circle the word 'kill' above. It's a very strong word. What you say can kill someone's dreams, devastate their self-esteem, take out their reputation and destroy any hope they have. That's what complaining does. Complaining is the secret killer of relationships.

Now circle the word 'life'. Words can give life - What you say can give someone joy, peace and hope through compliments. Your words can uplift someone who is going through a difficult time. Your words can bring hope to someone's life. And that is exactly what Paul does while he is sitting in prison. In a situation he can't change, a situation he wishes was different, he chooses the one thing that he can change: words. And you can choose to change your words too!

Rarely do we think about the power our words have. Notice the two words that Proverbs 18:21 ends with:

'you choose.' You can choose for your words to bring joy. You are 100% in control of your words. You may be struggling right now. Things may be hard, and you may be going through rough terrain, deep waters, or uncharted territory. What I'm asking you is: Will you choose to use words to uplift people, even if you are going through difficult times? Honestly, that is actually going to not just help them – that choice is going to help *you*. It will help reframe the way you see your circumstances. You can choose words that give life, and you'll be amazed at how that choice will give you life as well.

Complaining is the secret killer of our relationships.

There are three important reasons why we have to avoid complaining:

COMPLAINTS KILL GRATITUDE
Complaining about what you don't like keeps you from seeing all the things God has given you. Complaining about all the things that you don't have keeps you from seeing all the blessings around you. You can see, you can hear; and if you live in America, then you are automatically in the top 20% in the world regarding living conditions. Complaining about how much money you want to make causes you to forget that 80% of the

world lives on less than $1 a day. When you complain about how far you have to go in your career, goals, or pursuits, you forget how far God has brought you and all that He has done for you.

Remember Moses? He looks a lot like Charlton Heston, right? He parts the Red Sea and sets the people free from slavery in Egypt. Powerful! What a blessing! So much to be grateful for! These people have been saved from the bondage of slavery, they have Moses as their leader, and they are now in the wilderness headed to the Promised Land. It is only an 11 day journey to a different life. What could possibly go wrong? Here comes the secret killer . . .

> *The whole community of Israel complained about Moses and Aaron. "If only the Lord had killed us back in Egypt," they moaned. "There we sat around pots filled with meat and ate all the bread we wanted. But now you have brought us into this wilderness to starve us all to death."*
> (Exodus 16:2-3)

The Israelites complained about Moses! All he could do was part water – he's a horrible leader! He's the worst! Moses freed them from slavery! And yet, they complained – they would rather be back in Egypt? Had they forgotten that they were slaves back there? The conditions were horrible! They were beaten, they were starved to death, and even their young children were sometimes killed. But now, in the wilderness, all they remember is eating pots filled with meat and bread until they were full?! Do you see how complaining tends to rewrite your own history to support a negative attitude? *"We were treated great as slaves."* Who are they kidding? No they weren't!

Stop complaining. Take a moment right now and look around – find things to thank God for. You may be in difficult days right now, that's Real Life. But there is still so much good, so many blessings, to be found. This includes God's presence and God's peace, His promises, His sustaining love and grace, and that's just a start. Right now, I challenge you, stop reading this book and make a list of things that you can be thankful for. This exercise alone will keep you from complaining and move you back to gratitude.

Life is like a train track – two lines running parallel moving the same direction. There are blessings every day – that is one line of the track. There are also burdens every day – the other line of track. Real Life has burdens and blessings running parallel to each other. Each day has both - you choose which line you stare at – focusing on blessings moves you to be thankful.

However, complaints kill gratitude. There is a second thing that complaints kill:

COMPLAINTS KILL GENEROSITY

If you tell me how much you give to your local church, I'll tell you how much you struggle with complaining. If you don't give at least a tithe, this is a huge warning light and this is why: Complaining keeps you from being generous. Complaining says, "I am not content with what God has given me. I need to hold onto what I have, and I also want more for myself." Complaining and comparing lead to holding on tighter to what we have been given because we don't have faith that God will continue to provide generously for us.

This story about Mary is powerful. Mary was forgiven many times, saved by grace, totally forgiven. And she is so grateful. Gratitude moves us to generosity.

> *Then Mary took a twelve-ounce jar of expensive perfume made from essence of nard, and she anointed Jesus' feet with it, wiping his feet with her hair. The house was filled with the fragrance. But Judas Iscariot, the disciple who would soon betray him, said, "That perfume was worth a year's wages."*

(How great that Mary gave her yearly salary to Jesus! Nope, Judas is not celebrating generosity,

because he is a complainer.)

**It should have been sold and the money
given to the poor."**

*(Judas is complaining that Mary gave so sacrifi-
cially and selflessly to Jesus. Watch how the Bible
tells you what is really going on; Judas is trying to
sound all spiritual. We find out the truth here.)*

**Not that he cared for the poor - he was a thief,
and since he was in charge of the disciples'
money, he often stole some for himself.**
(John 12:3-6 NLT)

Did you know that when you are generous, someone is
always going to be there to complain? They might say,
"You're a little too excited about Jesus right now! Are
you sure you want to do that? Are you sure you want
to give that much to your church?" or "You sure are
reading your Bible a lot!" and "If you make one more
post on Facebook with a Bible quote, I tell you what..."
There is always someone who is going to complain
about your generosity and about how much you want
to lean in to gratitude and obedience.

Judas doesn't want to be generous with Jesus, because
he's all about himself. He wants to see how much he
can impress people and make them think he cares

about giving and being generous. He is all about how much he can collect for himself and not about what he can give.

Judas worked in the financial office of Jesus' ministry, but he wasn't generous. He never checked his complaining spirit. He sold Jesus out for 30 pieces of silver. Life for him was about what he could get. Life is empty when you make it about getting. Selfishness was literally a dead end road for Judas, but we can make a different choice.

Don't make life about what you can get – make life about what you can give. Don't let complaining rob you of being generous. The more you complain, the less generous you are because you are being selfish, self-centered, and holding on instead of letting go. The more generous you are, the less you complain.

Complaining focuses on what you don't have – generosity focuses on all God is giving you and how much others are in need. Complaining causes you to forget that there are others who are much more in need than you are. Through Paul's letter to the Phillipians, even though he is suffering, he reaches out to help others who are struggling, because it brings joy to his life. Complainers are not generous, but when you choose to bring life, you choose to help people who have a lot more needs than you do. And this brings joy not just to them but to your own heart!

Here is another thing that complaints kill:

COMPLAINTS KILL RELATIONSHIPS

If you want to have a miserable life and miserable relationships, just complain. It won't just affect your relationships with other people, it will affect your relationship with Jesus. Look what happens to Martha:

> *Jesus came to a certain village where a woman named Martha welcomed Him into her home. Her sister, Mary, sat at the Lord's feet, listening to what He taught. But Martha was distracted by the big dinner she was preparing. She came to Jesus and said, "Lord, doesn't it seem unfair to you that my sister just sits here while I do all the work? Tell her to come and help me."*
> (Luke 10:38-40)

Martha makes the choice many of us make, she invites Jesus into her life. However, then she gets distracted. Before we judge Martha, don't we do the same thing sometimes?

We welcome Jesus into our heart and into our home, and then we get distracted and complain about the people in our house. Can you imagine complaining about how spiritual your family is and saying, "Jesus, my family is spending too much time with you. Jesus, this is ridiculous." A complaining attitude is subtle and a secret killer.

Complaining is deadly. Complaining is a reflection of your own heart. From a negative heart overflows negative words, which generally become negative actions, which result in a miserable life. But if we are honest, we can all get distracted, like Martha. We can get distracted and miss what God's doing.

If you want to kill everything, complain about it. Do you want to kill your job? Then just complain about it. Complain about your commute; complain about the people that you work with who get on your nerves; complain about your boss who 'doesn't know anything'; complain about the lousy benefit package; and complain about how undervalued you are.

If you complain about your job, you will kill your job. And you will get fired.

Complaining kills everything that is the center of the complaint.

Complain about the weather, complain about the

economy, complain about your physical features, complain about the way people drive. Complain about gas prices. (Did you know that if you have a car, you are in the top 3% of the wealthiest people in the world?)[10]

You want to mess up your life? Complain about it.

Want to kill your marriage? Complain about it. You can mess up a perfectly good marriage by complaining. Find anything to complain about - big things and little things – they don't appreciate you, they chew their gum too loudly, they don't put their plates in the dishwasher, they never do the laundry, they leave all the errands for me to run.

You want to mess up your marriage? Do you want to kill a good marriage? Complain about it.

For those of you who are married, do you remember how it was when you were dating? You used to speak words of life: "I love you." "You are so good looking." "You are so nice to hang out with." Compliments! "When you walk into the room, the smoke detector goes off because you are so hot!" Compliments! "Are you tired? Because you have been running through my mind all day long." *We may be corny when we're in love, but at least we compliment each other and even go out of our way to do it!*

Once you are married for a while, somehow, those compliments turn into complaining and kill everything. Like this:

A long-time married couple is driving through the countryside. They drive by a farm with donkeys and pigs.

The wife says, "Relatives of yours?" And the husband, without any hesitation, replies, "As a matter of fact, yeah. My in-laws."

Why is it that we reserve our harshest words for the people we say that we love the most?

Why don't we communicate compliments more?

Want to destroy your family? Stop being intentional with your words. There was this survey once that asked children to share the number one thing they hear at home from their dad. The results?

1. "I'm too tired."

2. "We can't afford it."

3. "Quiet down."

It doesn't have to be this way! We can change the trend by protecting our homes and hearts from this secret killer. Remember, you get to choose. It's your choice to use compliments or complaining.

Everyone needs compliments; everyone needs affirmation. But most of the time, we are too busy complaining to give compliments.

Choose compliments – why? Let me offer four reasons. First of all ...

COMPLIMENTS ELEVATE YOUR INFLUENCE

Do you want to elevate your influence? Do you want to be a leader in your family, in your business, in your circle of friends? Are you tired of following the crowd?

Then decide right now that you are going to compliment everyone in your life. Every. Day.

Notice what Paul says right after his warning about complaining ...

> **Do everything without complaining and**
> **arguing, so that no one can criticize you.**
> **Live clean, innocent lives as children of God,**
> **shining like bright lights in a world full**
> **of crooked and perverse people.**
> (Philippians 2:14-15)

I love this analogy! When you choose to give life with your words it is like a bright light shining on a dark night. When you compliment someone, you are going to stand out like a bright star in a dark sky. Why do compliments stand out and shine? Because people just don't do it! Most people in our society are too busy complaining – not being generous, not being grateful – their selfishness is killing the relationships around them. But you can be different. You can push back the darkness with uplifting words that shine hope and life. Compliments will broaden your influence.

Do you want to be elevated at your job? Do you want to elevate your influence with your family? Elevate your influence with your friends? If Paul wrote a letter to the Philippians that read, 'Hard bed. Bad food. I quit,' no one would open the next letter he wrote. But when they get a letter about joy – 'shine like bright stars' – the people can't wait to get the next letter from him! Paul's influence reaches even to us 2,000 years later because he models his message: he chooses to encourage even in dark, discouraging times. In doing so he causes the people in Philippi to endear their hearts to his.

COMPLIMENTS STRENGTHEN RELATIONSHIPS
Compliments do the opposite of what complaints will do. They will strengthen your marriage. They will keep

your relationships healthy with your kids and with your co-workers. Compliments will strengthen your friendships.

Make the choice: compliment people! You might say, 'but at work, I have to give complaints because they aren't doing the work that's needed!' But if you ever need to give someone criticism, make sure it's in a *compliment sandwich*. Make sure that you have a compliment, and then what they need to work on, and then another compliment. Compliments allow the constructive cristicism to be easier to swallow.

A compliment can even be as easy as these two words: "Thank you!" Remember, being thankful protects you from falling into the quick sand of complaining.

Start being grateful today. Start by saying, "Thank you." Every day this week find somebody to say thank you to. Find something to say thank you for.

There's a story in the Old Testament about a difficult time in King David's life. His life went from bad to worse, because his son, Absalom, rebelled, formed an army, and went against his own dad. Absalom said, 'I'm king, and not you.' It was a horrific and bitter family feud. King David sent his army out, led by his leader Joab.

King David's men fought bravely and, against all odds, crushed the rebellion. They did exactly what King David told them to do. However, in the battle, King David's men killed Absalom. Of course, when King David received this news, he was sad and began grieving the loss of his son.

When the soldiers returned victorious from the battle, David did not say, 'thank you,' because he could not see past the death of his own son. But Joab, the leader of his army, came to him privately and tells him that he has to stop complaining. (*This is a wonderful principle: when you need to correct someone, do it privately.*) Joab tells him that he has to get out of this negative rut. Joab challenges his king to compliment his troops, who did exactly what he asked of them. Look at what general Joab told King David:

> ***Now get up! Go out there and thank them for what they did. If you don't ... you won't even have one man left on your side tomorrow morning.***
> (2 Samuel 19:7 CEV)

This is great advice for all of us. Get up, go out there and be grateful. If you want to change your relationships – with your spouse, with your coworkers, with your friends – get up now and say, "Thank you!"

If you do not start complimenting people, you will be a lonely person. This is more than just liking someone's Facebook post, or re-tweeting from someone's Twitter; this is using your words to compliment and encourage and be positive and generous. This is looking someone in the eyes and saying, "Thank you."

This is huge. We don't think about it, but it's why families are disintegrating, why relationships don't last. Because there is not enough positive complimenting and encouraging going on! Complaining is a secret killer.

A while back, some psychologists actually did a study where they put microphones in houses. *(Can you imagine a microphone being in your house?)* They recorded every comment that was made in these houses, and they gathered this data for a month (every comment, every word, all communication collected and calculated). This is what they discovered: they found that in the average American home, negative comments and complaints outweighed positive comments and compliments 10 to one. Yep, you read that correctly - 10 to one!! Let's change that. **I want to challenge you this week to give 10 positive comments for every one negative thing you say.** Ten compliments for every one complaint.

I want to tell you that as a pastor, I get to be on the front lines of the biggest tragedies and the greatest triumphs life has to offer. I get to see babies hours after they're born. But I also get to be there at funerals when tears flow and loved ones are honored. This is my observation: We are great at giving compliments at funerals. "He was such a great guy." "She was such a neat lady." It's fascinating to me because the people we are honoring are not there. All I'm asking you to do is back up the timeline. Whatever you would say at the funeral - go ahead - say it right now. Go ahead and say it this week. If you love them, tell them. If you care about them, tell them. If you're praying for them, tell them. If there is something you appreciate about them, give the compliment. If you want to compliment them, then compliment them today! And if you want to complain, don't.

Let's turn this whole thing around and make it 10 compliments to one complaint. This is how it starts:

Pause every morning and allow God to encourage you. For me, I have discovered that I am more likely to encourage people after I pause. This is how Paul puts it:

May our Lord Jesus Christ himself and God our Father, who loved us and by His grace gave

> *us eternal encouragement and good hope,*
> *encourage your hearts and strengthen you in*
> *every good deed and word.*
> (*2 Thessalonians 2:16-17*)

Can we be honest? Complaints are easy to come up with arent they? But God has a better plan – compliments – an appropriate word at an appropriate time.

> *An anxious heart weighs a man down, but a kind*
> *word cheers him up.* (*Proverbs 12:25*)

Do you believe that? Do you believe that someone can actually be worried, weighed down, have a heavy heart about something, and someone could say something, and a word or two could actually lift their load and change their perspective?

It is absolutely true: when you compliment someone and actually say something kind to them or about them, it brings comfort.

COMPLIMENTS BRING COMFORT

Your words can actually comfort someone.

Proverbs 12:25 says that a person's heart can get "weighed down". This is the same word used of an ocean that is churning, which reminds me of a story ...

One day, Jesus and the disciples were crossing the Sea

of Galilee and a huge storm came up. Massive waves threatened to sink their ship. Jesus had fallen asleep in the back of the boat. They woke Jesus up and He spoke these words, "Peace be still" and the storm disappeared and the water was calm.

When you read stories like that, you may think, "I wish I could talk to a storm and tell it to be still." Every day, there are anxious people all around us, and your words can stop the internal churning; you can comfort them with a compliment. Your words have power. Use the power of your words to bring comfort to those around you.

Do you comfort people with your words? You can. Every day. You can calm the storm in their hearts.

Another reason we should choose compliments:

COMPLIMENTS LEAD TO MOTIVATION
Words can actually motivate people to try things and accomplish things they otherwise wouldn't think they could achieve. Have you ever seen a child trying to ride a bike for the first time? It's new and unfamiliar, even a little scary. They want to do it so badly, but there is the fear of falling down and scraping their legs and hands that creeps up in the back of their minds. How is that child able to overcome that fear and believe in them-

selves enough to peddle faster and keep peddling after their parent has let go? It is because her dad is right behind her, shouting words of encouragement. "You've got this! Keep peddling! You're amazing!" Words. Powerful words from a loved one.

When someone is anxious about life and not very confident in their ability – a kind word can actually cheer them up, move them forward and motivate them to go further than they could have ever imagined on their own.

What do your words motivate people to do?

Compliments are a sign of genuine caring, not just about where a person is but where they can be. Compliments speak above current problems to a person's potential. True compliments are rooted in LOVE. God created every one of us in His image. And He instructed us to love others as we love ourselves. When we love the people in our lives, we compliment them. What better way to show love than to compliment someone else and therefore motivate them to fulfill the plan that God has for their lives.

> **Knowledge puffs up, but love builds up.**
> (*1 Corinthians 8:1*)

Words can build up courage and motivation in someone's heart. I call this "speaking into someone's life". Think about a hammer. Anyone can tear something down with a hammer, right? But it takes some skill and some time to actually build something with that hammer. Love can build up. Love is the foundation of a genuine compliment. When you pay someone a compliment, it costs you something. Encouragement takes energy out of you. You have to invest time and effort to write the letter, type the email, pick up the phone. On top of all this, a compliment takes attention off of you and places it on someone else. It's not easy, but when you love someone, then it is worth it!

Compliments are hard to do – complaining is easy.

Have you heard of Benjamin West? Even if you don't know his name, I'm sure you have seen his work, which is in schoolbooks and museums everywhere. This British painter's first picture almost ended in disaster. One day, when he was a young boy, his mother went out for a somewhat lengthy period of time to run some errands, leaving him in charge of his little sister, Sally. In his mother's absence, he discovered several bottles of colored ink, and so he decided that he would paint Sally's portrait. He ended up making a huge mess, with ink blots splashed all over the room and on the furniture. Soon after, his mother returned. She saw the mess but she said nothing. Instead, she picked up the piece of paper, saw the drawing, and then she said, "Why, it's Sally!" and stooped down and kissed Benjamin. From that moment on, Benjamin West would say, "My mother's kiss made me a painter."

If you love people – you can find something to compliment. Even through the paint-covered room, find the compliment – and encourage someone.

Start today. Be a bright and shining star in your circles of influence. Impact those around you by giving compliments, encouraging them, and lifting them up. This one act will create a ripple effect of motivation in your friendships and community that will be clearly visible.

Choose to pray these words to help avoid the silent killer of complaining:

PRAYER:
Lord, change my heart. Make me grateful. Make me generous. And make me an encourager. Lord, I know that as my heart changes, my words will also change. Like Paul, I may be struggling. Like Martha, I may feel like I am undeserving, but Lord, I pray peace and contentment over my life. No matter what my circumstances currently

are, Lord, help me to not complain. Help me to shine this week. I pray that Your light and love would shine in my heart and in my home, that it would shine in my workplace, and even shine in my social media platforms. I pray that my words will bring life as I choose to shine and be a light for you. Lord, thank you for all your blessings. Amen.

THE SECRET KILLER

"

*Pleasant words are a honeycomb,
sweet to the soul and healing
to the bones.*

"

(Proverbs 16:24)

4

HONEYCOMB

Words are everywhere. Think about how many ways we impact people with our words, and not just verbally. Think of the many different ways that you said something to somebody this week; verbally or maybe by texting, emailing, or on social media. This chapter is called *Honeycomb* because, just as honey is a healthy part of any diet, our words are meant to bring health and life to those who hear them. Healthy words (words said at the right time, in the right way, for the right reason) create healthy relationships.

We already know how many words that men and women each use every day. But, think about the different settings in which you use words each day. When you decide to change your words, and the purpose of your words, many things will be affected. By choosing to use the power of your words to encourage and lift up people in every area of your life, all your relationships – from family to friends to coworkers to your social media connections – will also be changed for the better. Words have that much power.

An older woman in a great big Cadillac was trying to get into a very tight parking space at a shopping mall in Dallas, Texas, and she didn't have the right angle to do so. She put her big car in reverse and backed up so that she could swing out wide and drive in straight.

Can you guess what happened? A young guy in a little red sports car shot right in front of her and took that parking space! The woman in the Cadillac was furious. "Hey, young man," she yelled out of her window. "What are you doing? Why did you take my parking space? You stole my spot!" And the young guy, getting out of his little car, just laughed and waved, and said, "I did it because I'm young and I'm fast!" And with that comment, he went into the store.

Well, he had been in the store for only a few minutes looking around, when suddenly he heard this awful crash outside. And as he ran toward the window to look out, wondering what in the world that noise could possibly be, he saw an astonishing sight: the old woman in the Cadillac had reared back and driven her car right into his! And not only that, but she was backing up and getting ready to do it again and again! She'd started to pound his car to pieces. The young guy couldn't believe it! He ran outside waving his hands at the old woman and yelling at her to stop. "What is wrong with you? Why are you doing this to my car?" The woman's reply? "Because I'm old and I'm rich!"

It's awful how we can do hurtful things to each other, isn't it? Sometimes it's on accident, but sometimes it's on purpose! With our words, we are shattering people to pieces.

Let's talk about the choice to heal people with our words.

I want you to look at a verse that we all need to take in. All of us need this verse. Every dad needs to apply this verse. Every mom needs to take this verse to heart. Every child needs to put this verse into practice. This one verse can change every relationship in your life:

> **Thoughtless words can wound as deeply as any sword, but wisely spoken words can heal.**
> (Proverbs 12:18 GN)

What you say can cause wounds worse than a blade.

And what you say can bring healing more powerful than any medicine in the world. That's how powerful your words are. 'Thoughtless' means to say something without thinking about it.

Have you ever said something, and once it came out of your mouth, you wish you could grab it and put it back in? Have you ever sent an email and then in an instant knew that you shouldn't have sent it? Or posted something and then regretted it right away, but it already got 135 likes?

Another word for thoughtless is reckless. To be reckless means, 'I'm not going to think about it and just let it happen without worrying about the consequences.'

It's like when you are driving a car and you kind of zone out – you stop thinking about what you are doing.

Are you a very responsible driver – have never been in an accident, or never even had a speeding ticket?

Or have you caused an accident or had a speeding ticket - maybe while driving a little reckless?

When we drive recklessly, we are going to have accidents. We're in this automobile that can really hurt people. But in the moment, we don't value the power and the responsibility of driving the vehicle, because, well, we just *have* to send this text right now! We have to plug the phone in to charge. We have to reach back and grab the toy that our child dropped on the floor. We have to speed even if it's raining. Sometimes we've got to do all these things at the same time! We have all been, at one time or another, a little careless with our vehicles. These are the reckless things we can do as drivers that can unintentionally cause a lot of damage to those around us when they lead to an accident.

Reckless words are like driving a vehicle irresponsibly. What you say – if it's thoughtless or reckless, if you don't pay attention, if you don't think about what you are saying – your words can actually result in a lot of damage. Reckless words cause a lot of hurt even if you didn't intend for it to happen.

Has someone ever hurt you with their words? Maybe something they said behind your back or even to your face? Thoughtless and reckless words can hurt.

Have you ever hurt someone with your words, behind their back or to their face?

If you are married – just go to your spouse and say "I'm sorry" right now – that will clear up a lot because we have all been thoughtless and reckless with how we speak to our spouse.

We are all wounded.

Hurt is everywhere. All of us have been hurt by someone, and all of us have hurt someone.

Because we all live in an imperfect world, you are going to get hurt. You will be hurt by accidents and illnesses, but the deepest hurts you will experience in your life will come from people. Can people hurt you? Oh yes – and you can hurt people. The deepest wounds in your life will come from your interactions with people.

Relationships should be and are the source of life's greatest blessings. If you think about it, that is where joy comes from – that's what it's all about – the people in our lives. However, not only are relationships the source of our greatest joy; some of the greatest hurt in our lives also comes from these same relationships.

Let's look back at the Israelites as they flee from Egypt. God's people are going to say some hurtful things to Moses – on purpose.

Moses stood up to Pharaoh, the most powerful ruler in the world at that time, and told him to "Let God's people go." God delivered the people from slavery and

Pharaoh let them leave with Moses. They were on their way to the Promised Land! They were camping at the shore of the Red Sea when all of a sudden, someone spotted Pharaoh's army coming on the horizon. Pharaoh had changed his mind and the Egyptian Army was chasing the Israelites, and the people could see the army coming! It doesn't take a rocket scientist to know that chariots are faster than walking – it would not take long for the Egyptians to catch up to them.

With this looming crisis and the emotional panic this threat causes, thoughtless words gush out . . .

As Pharaoh approached, the people of Israel looked up and panicked when they saw the Egyptians overtaking them. They cried out to the Lord, and they said to Moses,

(it's always somebody else's fault)

"Why did you bring us out here to die in the wilderness? Weren't there enough graves for us in Egypt? What have you done to us? Why did you make us leave Egypt?

(Moses didn't make them leave Egypt – they were excited to go!)

Didn't we tell you this would happen while we were still in Egypt?

(no, no one said anything – everybody was 'all in' for following Moses)

> *We said, 'Leave us alone! Let us be slaves*
> *to the Egyptians. It's better to be a slave in*
> *Egypt than a corpse in the wilderness!'"*
> (*Exodus 14:10-12*)

Those are some hurtful words. How would you respond to someone saying things like, 'Why did you do that?' or 'Look what you have done!' or 'I told you this was going to happen,' or even, 'Leave me alone!'

Doesn't just reading this passage make your blood boil a bit? Are you feeling ready to tell them off, yet? These were God's chosen people saying these reckless things. This was God's family on the verge of freedom and a new life in the Promised Land – and words are about to tear them apart. Moses has a choice to make – will he react to what they are saying or will he choose to respond differently despite their toxic emotions and negative words?

We tend to slowly shift from positive to negative. From complimenting to complaining. From healthy to hurtful. From sweet to sour. One guy said, "In the first year of marriage, my wife used to bring me my slippers and the dog came barking. Now my dog brings me my slippers ..." You know where he was going with this, don't you? And I'd love to hear the wife's perspective on what's changed!

When two people choose to share healthy and healing words with each other, relationships can be awesome. However, when two people get into a rut of communicating with criticism and sarcasm, all of a sudden a relationship can become very unhealthy. If you are not careful, you may even try to isolate yourself from *all people* because you were hurt by *one person*.

This is an important issue. Don't miss this. You are designed to be in healthy relationships with other people. You are not designed to do life on your own. God designed you to connect to Him and his family known as the church. The solution to healthy relationships starts with you becoming healthy.

Good health begins when you open your heart to God and allow His Spirit to work in you. Love, joy, peace and patience are all you need to begin to speak healthy words to others. When you have a healthy connection to God and a growing relationship with Him, your connection to people will change. Relationships with people only work when words are healing. The goal of communication should be to produce healthy emotions. The change in your relatioinships starts with you getting healthy.

The Israelites were in community and following

Moses as a group. They were God's family going to the Promised Land. And, by the way, that's how you get to the Promised Land: together! We are going to become all God wants us to be when we are following him in healthy community: together. But watch what is tearing the Israelites apart: words! When words are unhealthy, take caution. Words tear relationships apart. Words tear families apart. Words tear friendships apart. Words tear coworkers apart.

We are created for community. We are wired for relationships. We were formed for a family. We are made to go through life together. Here's the problem. It's easy to get disconnected in relationships. It's very easy to get disconnected from your children, from your parents, from your brothers and sisters, your friends your family, your husband or wife. It's easy to get disconnected from your church, from your LifeGroup.

Why do relationships fall apart? Why do relationships go bad? What destroys relationships? Words. Hurtful words are said. Wounds are created. Resentment sets in. If we are not careful, we become bitter or infected with the same negativity, and we end up hurting other people as well.

Let me share a little secret with you – I want to warn you. Ready? **People are different than you.** Because of that, they are not going to always agree with you. And you know the only two people who agree on everything are two dead people. It's true.

We know we cannot agree on everything with another human being, because we're all imperfect. We all have different ways of doing things, different perspectives, and different feelings. Unfortunately, we're not taught how to have healthy relationships. We never had a class on that growing up in school; not a single class on how to have good relationships. Funny, isn't it? How to have good relationships is the most important thing in life. It's far more important than anything else – how to have a relationship with God, how to have a relationship with people.

Moses gives us a course on relationships. He shows us that he is 100% responsible for what he is about to say. These people are coming against him with some very hurtful words. And why? Because they are wounded! When someone is saying hurtful things to us, if we can just hit pause, if we can just remember what is really happening, it is going to help us choose to use our words in a healing way rather than a hurtful way.

Here are three things that Moses teaches us:

WHEN PEOPLE SAY HURTFUL THINGS, THEY ARE HURTING

The Israelites were saying these things to Moses because they were coming out of 400 years of slavery. 400 years! 400 years of abuse and mistreatment and abandonment. Have you ever heard the phrase, 'hurt people hurt people'? Absolutely true. They're hurting and they're coming after Moses now. But it's not Moses. If you can just remember when somebody is coming at you, it's not usually you – *they* are hurting inside. Whoever hurt you was hurting themselves.

If I have a wound on my hand and you come up to me to say, "Hi," and give me a firm handshake, not knowing I was wounded, you would be surprised when I smack you in the face and push you away from me. You would probably get mad because now I have hurt you and rejected you. You are unaware that I am wounded and the pain I'm feeling when you squeeze my hand causes me to go into fight or flight mode and protect myself. But if you don' know I am wounded, all you see is my hurtful reaction to you. Because I'm hurting, I am hurting you!

This principle can help you so much when you are in

an argument with a friend or spouse or coworker, because when they are yelling at you and are saying hurtful things, your tendency will be to say mean things back – but wait! Hold on. Pause. Recognize they are hurting. Instead of responding with hurt, show them compassion because they are wounded. Choose to bring healing into their lives.

Hurt people hurt people. People who are hurting tend to lash out and hurt others. We have to stop the cycle before the wounds destroy our relationships.

People get divorced over words. Families are torn apart over words. People lose jobs over words. When we forget we are all wounded, we only continue to wound others and we never make the powerful choice to allow our words to heal.

In school we learned to stop, drop, and roll. Moses wants us to learn something even more valuable. Stop, drop the hurtful comments, and remember when people say hurtful things, they are hurting.

Here is the second thing Moses teaches us:

WHEN PEOPLE CUT YOU DOWN, THEY HAVE A LOW SELF-ESTEEM

Many people have insecurity and a poor self-image because of words spoken to them. The people who were yelling at Moses and blaming, belittling and cutting him down, were told by their Egyptian task-masters for generations that they were worthless and less than human. The way they were treated as slaves caused them to lash out at Moses with the same demeaning words.

Your words are a reflection of you, and your heart, more than they are a reflection of the person you are talking to or talking about.

I met this person recently and they said, "Oh, you are Micah, the Pastor of Real Life? I ran into somebody who used to go to your church and they said [this and this and this] about you." They proceeded to give me a laundry list of rumors, and none of them were good. Do you know I wasn't even mad? Well, maybe I was upset for a second. But, fortunately, I was in the process of writing this chapter. I pushed pause. After I thought about it for a second, I actually felt sorry for the person who manufactured this negative list of items about me. People cut you down when they're down in their emotions and have a low self-esteem. I'm thankful to Moses for teaching me this lesson just in time.

Here is the third thing Moses teaches us:

WHEN PEOPLE SAY "LEAVE ME ALONE", THEY NEED HELP

These people say, "Moses, leave us alone." The irony is they need more help at that moment than they have ever needed. When you're at the grocery store on aisle 9, and your 5-year-old child yells, "Leave me alone! I wish you were never my parent. I don't ever want to see you again!" What do you do? Do you respond, "Okay. See ya. Good luck getting home!" No! Well, that may be what you wanted to say, but instead you choose your words because you can see beyond their words. What is the 5-year-old *really* saying? (If you listen beyond the words, you will hear.) "I need you. I don't know what to do right now. I'm frustrated. I'm scared. I'm really anxious!"

Remember this: when a person says, "Leave me alone," that is the moment they really need the most help. You can use your words to heal! Moses saw beyond the cutting words.

Words kill, words give life;
they are either poison or fruit – you choose.
(*Proverbs 18:21*)

You cannot choose how people talk to you, treat you, or what they say to you, but you can choose how you respond. You are 100% in control of your words. Moses chose his words. But before we look at what he said, what would you have said if someone told you that 'it's all your fault' … 'I told you this would happen' … 'I didn't want to be with you' … 'I wish I had never met you' … 'leave me alone'?

How would you be feeling if you were Moses? Well, while you are thinking about how you would have responded – let me tell you what I would say - if you catch me on the wrong day - before I've prayed in the morning. I would definitely be tempted to react, 'Oh, yeah. It is ON. Go on back to Egypt. Pharaoh's on his way to get you, so HA! Leave you alone? No problem! I'm about to part the Red Sea and I'm the only one who's going to walk through it!' Then I would part the water, walk across by myself and then yell back at the Isrealites and say, 'Bye, Felicia!'

But Moses shows us how it's done. Moses hits pause. Hedoesn't say the first thing that comes to mind. Even though he did struggle with anger, Moses doesn't let his emotions get control of his mouth. Moses chooses to bring life. The Israelites were trying to cut down and hurt with their words, but Moses gives us five principles that make our words like honeycomb. First of all, Moses teaches us that no matter what hurt people do or say …

WE CAN ALL HEAL

We are all wounded. But we can all heal. You can heal
– Yes, you. And this is a powerful thought: **You can
actually heal people with your words**. I want you to
hold on to that truth. It is a miraculous power! *You* can
actually bring healing to any relationship. Words can
transform any environment. Your decision to heal with
your words will change your relationships. It will
change your family. It'll change your work environment; it will change your office. It will change your
friendships. It'll change your Facebook. What you say
carries power, so hold onto that. Let's see how Moses
does it. Because today, I want Moses' words to heal *you*
so that you can heal *others* with your words.

Whatever wounds you have today, you can heal. Today
– no matter how you have been hurt – you can heal.

Let's go back to our story. The Israelites are trapped at
the Red Sea, and Moses is surrounded by wounded
people. Moses responds to the hurtful words with
healing. He speaks three phrases. Everybody listening
to his words or reading this chapter needs one of
these. I believe that we can all heal with the same
words that Moses gave to these people. God is giving
these words to you today.

But Moses told the people, "Don't be afraid.
Just stand still and watch the Lord rescue you
today. The Egyptians you see today will never be
seen again. The Lord himself will fight for you.
Just stay calm." (Exodus 14:13-14)

Can you feel the contrast? From the cynical words of
the people to the comforting words of the leader?
From hurtful words to healing words? The things that
Moses says to the people are the same things God is
saying to you today and how you can use your words
to help others. Moses teaches us this principle:

MY WORDS HEAL WHEN THEY BRING YOU BACK TO THE PRESENT

Moses tells them, "Don't be afraid."

Moses draws them back to this: I'm here and I'm still
alive. I know we're by this huge sea and it feels like a
crisis but God can bring a miracle!

Your enemy, the Devil, uses two things in your life to
draw you back in the wrong direction: worry and guilt.
Worry keeps dragging you into the future. The enemy
doesn't know what's going to happen in the future any
more than you do. But he says he can tell you what it's
going to be. It's going to be this. And it's going to be
terrible and you're going to do this wrong. You're going

to be a slave and there's no way Pharaoh isn't going to catch up with you. The enemy takes you into a future that you don't know, but it's a future that God has and He is in control.

If the Devil can't get you to go into the future with your thoughts, he'll get you to go back to the past. Guilt keeps tugging you into the past. "Remember you were a slave, right? Your dad was a slave, his dad was a slave. You will never be free, you'll never change, you'll never get to the Promised Land. You'll never get to where God wants you to go." And the enemy will remind you of your past and stack up all your mistakes as reasons your future will not be good. That's called guilt.

The enemy either uses worry or guilt to keep you from being in the moment - right here in the present. But guess what God can do with guilt: Forgive. Are you ready for a new beginning? Are you ready to go some-where else? Are you ready to not be a slave anymore? Because I have a Promised Land for you. Because of Jesus, all has been forgiven. We don't deserve it. We can't earn it. But He gives it to us freely.

Worry? I don't have to worry about it, I just have to pray about it. God's already in the future. That's why today is called the present; it's a gift.

Moses tells God's people:

> **The Lord himself will go before you. He will
> be with you; He will not leave you or forget
> you. Don't be afraid and don't worry.**
> *(Deuteronomy 31:8)*

The phrase, 'don't be afraid' shows up in the Bible 365
times – that's one for every day of the year! He has
a 'don't be afraid' for every day of your life. Don't be
afraid. Don't worry because worry blows the future
out of proportion. Worry keeps you from enjoying
today because you are so anxious about tomorrow.

Worrying always blows things out of proportion.

It reminds me of a video that recently went viral. More
than 500,000 people saw it. The video shows this giant
spider, the size of a large dog, creeping up behind a
police officer who was on a traffic stop, standing next
to the car and talking with the driver. A spider the size
of a dog – and an unknowing police officer just focused
on his job. What in the world?!

What was really fascinating was to watch the comments
on social media. Comments like, 'I knew there was
a spider that big - I was out in West Texas and there

were tarantulas out there and they were *huge*!' As the video continues, that huge spider comes from the grass over on the opposite side of the street, walks across the street, and literally walks up behind that police officer. On social media, people were just freaking out. 'Don't go outdoors! There're giant spiders out there! They're everywhere! These giant spiders are attacking police officers! Tarantulas have gone crazy and are taking over the world!'

It turns out that the 'giant spider' was actually a tiny spider walking on the police officer's windshield. And it walked right in front of the camera on his dash that was recording the traffic stop. The camera created an optical illusion and blew up the size of the spider to where it looked like it was about 3-feet tall. When I saw this video, I thought: that's how worry works!

Worry amplifies everything that could go wrong. 'Don't go outside! There are spiders out there that are attacking police officers!' Did you know psychologists have discovered that 90% of what you worry about doesn't even come true? Listen. Don't be afraid. It's going to be okay. That spider is actually, well, the size of a spider. And in God's eyes, everything is that small!

Worry weights a person down; an encouraging word cheers a person up. (*Proverbs 12:25*)

Do your words bring anxiety or do they soothe? Words have the power to cheer up and can be like honeycomb.

Here is the third principle that Moses teaches us:

MY WORDS HEAL WHEN THEY BRING YOU BACK TO TRUST IN GOD

The Israelites had an Egyptian army on the horizon in one direction, and in the other, the Red Sea. Moses tells them, *"Watch the Lord rescue you today."* God is saying the same thing to you today. He is going to come through for you. You need to trust him with your situation.

You're going to overcome your obstacles - it's going to be okay. You can trust God with every trouble in your life, big or small. If it is big enough to worry about, it is big enough to pray about. God cares about everything happening in your life.

This is a good time to pause in our journey to say, if you have never trusted in Jesus to be your Lord and Savior, now is the perfect time to do that. You can trust God for your salvation. You can trust Him and He can come and live in your heart. He is the way to heaven. If you have never received Jesus, you need to do that. Trust Him right now. How? Just whisper this prayer:

God forgive me and save me. Jesus, I believe you died on the cross and rose again, so right now, come live in me. I don't know everything but I do know I need you. I turn from this world and turn everything over to you. I want to follow you the rest of my life and thank you for the promise of heaven! In Jesus' name, Amen.

If you just prayed that prayer, congratulations! Please let your pastor or a leader in your church know. Find a church that teaches the Bible and stay connected to that church family! Four things that you must do to grow as a Christian: Attend the worship service, find a small group, find a place to serve the church, and give money to that church, because where your treasure is, that is where your heart will be. Keep your heart focused on God and His family by investing your time, talent and treasure in God's family.

Okay, back to trusting God with everything you face. If you are already a Christian and have Jesus in your life and know you are going to heaven, let me ask you a question: If you are trusting God to get you to heaven after you die, what could you possibly be worried about in this temporary life? To trust God with your eternity - that's the biggest leap ever, right? And if He's got that, which He does, then let Him be the one you trust with everything.

> *I pray that from his glorious, unlimited resources, He will empower you with inner strength through his Spirit. Then Christ will make his home in your heart as you trust in Him. Your roots will grow down into God's love and keep you strong.* (Ephesians 3:16-17)

Allow the decision to trust God to take root in your own heart. I pray that your heart will be a place of trust and peace in your life. When we trust God, we have the love and strength to motivate others to trust Him as well. We can heal others when we encourage them: "Trust God to take care of you today."

The fourth principle we learn from Moses about healing words is:

EVERY WORD YOU SAY MOVES PEOPLE TOWARD GOD OR AWAY FROM HIM

Moses moves the people toward God with his words. And your words will either move people toward God or move them away from Him. Every comment does.

> *Pleasant words are a honeycomb, sweet to the soul and healing to the bones.* (Proverbs 16:24)

Do you know what honeycomb is? Some of you grew up eating Honeycomb cereal. This verse is not about cereal. Honeycomb is a structure of hexagonal cells made by bees to store honey. It actually has more properties to help your nutrition and health than I could possibly cover here. But here are a few things:

Allergies. Chewing honeycomb for 30 minutes can stop all allergy symptoms including sneezing, runny nose and watery eyes.

Skincare. Honeycomb can be incredible for skincare and as a facial moisturizer. It can heal scarring and many other skin infections.

Home Remedies. Honey has been used for many years to treat arthritis pain, sore throats, insomnia and as a natural cure for cuts and burns.

It sounds like we all need to chew on some honeycomb right now! But before you go buy some, let' think about what this verse is telling us. Here's the point: words have more healing power than you can possibly imagine. Your words can actually heal someone's soul.

Words can be a remedy. Everyone around you is wounded. How are you going to heal their wounds? This Scripture is saying your words are like honeycomb. 'How am I am going to fix this relationship? How can I fix this friendship? or How can I fix this problem with our relationship?' Start with words. What you say can actually soothe someone's soul. Pleasant words are like honeycomb; they can give hope. Words can hurt, but they can also heal!

Words bring hope. Let these words I write bring hope to you right now. There is hope for your family. There is hope for your marriage. There is hope for your kids. There is hope for your struggle. There is hope in your hardship. There is hope for your life.

Choose to be like honeycomb.

Moses moves the people toward God. His words are like honeycomb. He brings them hope.

There is also a fifth thing that Moses teaches us:

MY WORDS HEAL WHEN THEY BRING YOU BACK TO PEACEFUL QUIET

Most of the time we try to bring peace and quiet by yelling, "Calm down! Be quiet! Everybody stop talking! Shut your mouth!" Although yelling is not effective, we are screaming what our heart desires: peace and stillness.

In Exodus 14:14, Moses tells the people simply, *"Just stay calm."*

Moses gives us a great example here: he tells them to be calm in an effective way. They were panicking, running around not staying focused. Moses tells them not to panic. Sometimes the best thing you can do is to PAUSE.

Pausing allows you to step back and determine what really matters. Does this really matter? You can pause and ask God to draw your heart to what does matter. I had a friend send me a pic of the sunrise just this morning. It was absolutely stunning. Looking at God's creation reminded me to PAUSE. And think about the words I could use today to heal. To bring me back to a peaceful quiet.

Think about it this way. New Orleans Saints quarterback Drew Brees made his way into the NFL record books recently with a 62-yard touchdown pass to break the all-time NFL passing yards record (71,968!). But the most played highlight from the game was not of him throwing the winning pass. The most replayed highlight of Drew Brees' record-breaking evening was what he did *after* he completed the pass. The game was still going on, and his family was on the sidelines to celebrate the accomplishment with him ESPN's microphones picked up an unbelievably heartfelt exchange between Drew and his sons. He hugged his three sons, Baylen, Bowen and Callen, and told them that they can accomplish anything. He said, "I love you guys so much. You can accomplish anything in life that you're willing to work for. Alright?"

That's what matters. I mean, what he did was like throwing a football from California all the way to New York and back. And the best thing he's going to do is encourage his boys. Why? Because Drew Brees was told 'you're too short.' 'You don't have a good enough running game.' 'You can't throw this way.' 'You'll never make it in the NFL.' Because he didn't let those hurtful words go down into his heart. At this pinnacle achievement of his career, he reminds all of us that, at the end of the day, we need to pause and go back to what really matters. And what really matters is your connection with God and the people that really say they love us and we really, deep down, love them.

If you could pause during an argument and someone could interview you and ask you what's going on, you would take a breath, and you would say, "Well, I really love this person, but I'm wounded, so I'm yelling at them." PAUSE. I need to take a moment and choose that I will not hurt with my words today.

*Encourage one another and build each
other up, just as in fact you are doing.*
(*1 Thessalonians 5:11*)

This word - encourage - in Hebrew is the word Parakaleo:

Parakaleō - **to give support, confidence, hope and
comfort.**

This same word is used to describe the Holy Spirit
and is the same principle we need to apply in bringing
peace to our relationships. The word means 'to come
alongside.' It means to be peacefully present with each
other and bring support, encouragement, hope and
comfort. Do you know how you can do this? PAUSE.

Sometimes, the best thing you can say is nothing.
This principle is especially true for those of you who
just want to fix it. Maybe the best thing you can do
sometimes is just PAUSE and simply be there in the
present moment. By doing so, you can bring comfort
and care. That pause is what helps bring a peaceful
quiet to the whole situation. I would encourage you to
PAUSE this week and see God for who He is.

Notice the first two words of this verse:

*BE STILL **and know that I am God!***
(*Psalm 46:10*)

This is a lost art in American culture. I'm going to ask you right now just to be still and let this reality sink in: *No matter how you are feeling or what anyone else is saying, there is hope.*

This is what Moses is telling God's people – there is hope. This is what God is telling you – there is hope for your marriage. There is hope for your family. There is hope in that situation. There is hope! That obstacle you are facing is only an opportunity for God to deliver you. There is hope and that spider is really a speck on the windshield. There's hope and God has a promised land waiting for you. You are His child and He's going to take care of you.

PRAYER:
Heavenly Father, help me to be still and know that you are God. Remind me of how powerful you are. Thank you for loving me. Thank you for taking care of me. Help me to be aware of your Presence and give me your Peace. I trust you with everything.

HONEYCOMB

"

He who covers over an offense promotes love, but whoever repeats the matter separates close friends.

"

(Proverbs 17:9)

5

70x7

Not too long ago in Austin, there was a water problem due to an unexpected amount of rain. It had rained to the point where the city's water filtration systems were compromised. The city of Austin issued a city-wide boil water notice and people were warned not to drink the water. Everyone panicked and there was a run on bottled water as people tried to make sure they would not run out.

Whether you've experienced this yourself or not, just trust me: When water is scarce, it is not good! This was a new experience for Austin, because it rarely has water quality issues. It had gotten so bad that, wait for it - Starbucks and other coffee shops shut down for days! A city without a coffee shop... I have no idea how we survived. Many people barely made it. The hunt for bottled water reached doomsday proportions and people became so eager to get their hands on as many cases of bottled water as they could that some stores had to limit the purchase to one case per household. All of this due to a shortage of what we needed. We needed clean water!

As soon as people think there's going to be a scarcity – when there is a shortage of any kind – people tend to panic. Anxiety is a little high. Emotions elevate, our lives are strained and there is stress and worry because we are not getting what we need.

Today I want to focus on another shortage – one more serious than not getting bottled water. It's something you need more than food and water. You don't realize it, but when there is a shortage of this, your relationships get strained and stressed and there is worry, anxiety, and tension, and you probably don't even realize where it is coming from. The world is in desperate need of it. And when there is a scarcity of this, we know we need *something*, but we don't know what it is that is missing. We look for the fix in self-help books, love songs, busy-ness or podcasts. When there is a scarcity, there is a panic. We know there is something missing; we just can't pinpoint what it is. In fact, God designed us to pursue it, so that we can not only find it ourselves, but also so that we can share it with others.

What is it? FORGIVENESS.

Forgiveness is a very powerful word. I believe in America today, the need for forgiveness is very high, but the supply is very low. As a matter of fact, have you ever asked anyone for forgiveness? Think back to that time – was it a teacher, a parent, a coworker, maybe it was a friend? – when you asked for forgiveness from some-one, and they forgave you. How did that make you feel? I'm guessing it felt pretty good, didn't it?

Have you ever asked someone to forgive you and they chose not to?

Let's flip the coin here - has anyone come to you seeking forgiveness and you chose not to forgive them?

> *Don't use foul or abusive language. Let everything you say be good and helpful, so that your words will be an encouragement to those who hear them. And do not bring sorrow to God's Holy Spirit by the way you live. Remember, He has identified you as his own, guaranteeing that you will be saved on the day of redemption. Get rid of all bitterness, rage, anger, harsh words, and slander, as well as all types of evil behavior.*
> *(Ephesians 4:29-31)*

Before we get to the bitterness and harsh words that forgiveness can wash away, let's unpack the first sentence of this passage. Ephesians is telling us not to use foul or abusive language. Take that phrase to heart, and I guarantee it'll change your life. We live in an absolutely crude culture. Remember when it used to be a big deal when a movie had just five F-bombs in it? Now, as long as there are less than a hundred, we consider it to be a good family-friendly movie! Our world is literally inundated with foul and abusive language. We need a different F-word – **we need Forgiveness!**

Have you noticed how many times the name of Jesus is taken in vain by people around you or in movies? And have you noticed that nobody takes any other religious leader's name in vain? I've never been to a movie where a guy gets shot in the leg and he shouts, "Buddha!" In an action thriller, no one ever gets frustrated and yells, "Confucious!" It's always a slight on the name of Jesus. There is definitely an agenda, by the world, created by the enemy (and we only have one enemy) and the agenda is clear: 'just say whatever you want!' And because we are hearing this on a daily basis, we become numb to its effects and we no longer notice when we even take Jesus' name in vain ourselves. Ironically, **Jesus is the source of forgiveness.**

This passage gives us three filters for our words. First: *"Don't use foul or abusive language."* I've had many teenagers ask me how we know what's even a foul word? Who decided what words are bad? Next: *"Let everything you say be good and helpful, so that your words will be an encouragement to those who hear them."* Before you say something, ask yourself this: Is it good? Is it helpful? That's the test. If you answer 'no' to those questions, but you still feel like you need to get it off your chest, then go to the third filter: *"And do not bring sorrow to God's Holy Spirit by the way you live."* This is a great question to ask before you speak: will what I say bring sorrow to God? Allow these three statements to be filters before you open your mouth. If your words don't make it throught these three filters, swallow them and keep them to yourself.

When you receive Jesus into your life, He is going through the day with you. And when you are thinking about saying something, you will sense an internal whisper – Jesus will say, 'No, don't say that!' When we say it anyway, then we are going against the One who is inside of us, the One who is guiding us, the One who wants to give us the strength to live a different life. When we go against Him, it grieves Him, inside of us. *"Remember, He has identified you as his own, guaranteeing that you will be saved on the day of redemption."*

Remember, you are His child! So, live like it and speak like it!

The alternative to forgiveness is found in verse 31: *"Get rid of all bitterness, rage, anger, harsh words, and slander, as well as all types of evil behavior."* This is a great list about the negative effects of words. When you don't deal with your heart and don't check your words, this is what happens: your words become abusive and foul when you are bitter and angry. We can get stuck in the loop of bitterness, or we can break the loop. When we ignore the decision to forgive, we tear down the people around us. Instead of being forgivers, we become faultfinders.

Faultfinders have three destructive habits. First, faultfinders don't get rid of bitterness, instead:

FAULTFINDERS TEAR DOWN RELATIONSHIPS.
People who are faultfinders are miserable people who make everyone else miserable, too. Because they are filled with resentment and anger, all they have to share in their relationships are harsh words that slander and tear down. Forgiveness is the only remedy to the wrecking ball of abusive words.

The Bible says don't use foul or abusive language, use words that are good and helpful; make sure your words build people up. Let's go back to the analogy of our words being like a hammer. Can a hammer do good things or things that hurt? Both! We've all seen the movies where a bad guy uses a hammer to do serious damage, right? But a hammer can also build an entire house! It can really do some good. And this hammer can also tear a whole house down. That is how powerful your words are. Forgiveness is one of the key materials in building a great relationship.

Why should you forgive? Well, go through the filters of Ephesians 4: is this going to be good? Absolutely. Is this going to be helpful? Yes! It is so needed. Will this please God? Yes! Remember, He is the source of it. Forgiveness is good and helps the people around you, but it also helps YOU! Bitterness, anger and revenge can eat you up inside. **What is the best thing that you can do for you? Forgive.**

This is your decision every day: forgive or find fault. Using encouraging words and offering forgiveness is something you get to decide. Faultfinders don't care. Because there are so many faultfinders, forgiveness is the scarcest word out there. Faultfinders refuse to forgive. They're going to tear down the relationship.

They refuse to forgive and instead, keep bringing up the mistakes. This dangerous habit of tearing down relationships leads to the second destructive pattern faultfinders have:

FAULTFINDERS BLAME EVERYONE ELSE.
Simply stated, faultfinders blame everyone else. Instead of forgiving, they point out why forgiveness is not deserved. A person who is faultfinding takes their mistakes and instead of asking for forgiveness, they find reasons why it is everybody else's fault.

The blame game... Yep, it's the oldest game in the world. It goes as far back as Adam and Eve. God created man and woman and put them in a perfect environment. His instructions were clear, "There's only one thing I do not want you to eat – don't eat from this one tree." He told them, "But look at all of these beautiful trees everywhere. You have so much blessing in your life. Just... don't eat from this one tree - don't do this one thing."

Have you ever sent a 3-year-old into a room and said, "You can play with anything in this room, just don't play with this outlet right here." What is the first thing the child heads for? The outlet! And that is exactly what happened to Adam & Eve, and it happens to all of us. We don't focus on all of God's blessings, and instead we look at that one thing, and that one thing brings us down.

Both Adam and Eve disobeyed and did what God told them NOT to do. They sinned. And all of a sudden, they were ashamed and they hid from God. He came to the garden to find them in this fallen state, with their rebellious hearts still resistant to his loving pursuit.

Who did God call first? He called on Adam – and look at how Adam responds:

> *The man said, "The woman you put here with me - she gave me some fruit from the tree, and I ate it." Then the LORD God said to the woman, "What is this you have done?" The woman said, "The serpent deceived me, and I ate."*
> (Genesis 3:12-13)

Adam takes it like a man and blames his wife! Then Adam actually blames God. He tells God, it isn't my fault - it's *your* fault. The woman blames the serpent. She says it isn't my fault – it's *their* fault.

Faultfinders never find forgiveness because they are so busy blaming others to realize that they need it. They blame their circumstances, their parents, their boss, even their family tree – "Well, what do you expect? I'm

Irish, so I just get angry! "It's not my fault; my ancestors made me this way." Really?

Faultfinders avoid their own weaknesses and shortcomings by continually pointing out everyone else's. They don't take responsibility for their actions or words, instead they use their words to blame others. This dangerous pattern leads to the most destructive habit of all:

FAULTFINDERS DIG UP THE PAST.
Faultfinders are great at digging. We've already learned that words are like a hammer, but they can also be a shovel. Faultfinders use words like a shovel, digging up things that destroy relationships. Faultfinders dig up things from the past instead of staying current.

When an argument starts, do you go and get the shovel and start digging? When the conflict heats up, do you find yourself white knuckling the shovel? "Where did I bury that hatchet? I know it's here somewhere!" If we aren't careful, we all do this. All of a sudden we find ourselves digging up things from the past instead of staying in the present. "Do you remember when you forgot this ... said this ... did this ..." Then the shovel strikes a landmine, "Well, 15 years ago ..." If we are not careful, our words dig up things from the distant past and suddenly, we're not living in the present. **When we dig up the past, we get bitter and angry, and we use harsh words.**

Avoid digging! Faultfinding kills relationships!

Now let me show you another verse in the Bible. Before reading this next verse, remember - the Bible is the inspired Word of God:

> **Better to live in a desert than with a quarrelsome and nagging wife.** (Proverbs 21:19 NIV)

Let's just meditate on that for a second. Isn't that the truth?!

Now ladies, don't be upset – I've got you covered. Check out this verse:

> *It is better to have an icepick in your eye, than to be married to a condemning, controlling and judgmental man. (2 Davidson 4:2)*

Amen! Am I right, ladies?

Wait - you didn't know there was a book called 2 Davidson in the Bible? That's because there isn't, of course, but that is still truth. Listen, guys. Listen, ladies. We all need to stop being faultfinders.

Now this verse IS in the Bible:

> *Words kill, words give life;*
> *they are either poison or fruit – you choose.*
> *(Proverbs 18:21 MSG)*

This is the main principle we are walking through. You don't get to choose your circumstances. You don't get to choose what someone says to you. You do, on the other hand, get to choose *how* you're going to respond with your words. Your words can bring life to situations, or your words can be condemning and judgmental. If you are not careful, your relationships can become a desert - just a dry, arid land where there is a scarcity of the word that is needed most. That word is forgiveness.

Let's make the choice to not be faultfinders. Don't be someone who walks around criticizing the relationship and missing all the blessings and all the good things that the relationship has to offer. Don't miss out on a lifelong friendship by holding on to the one thing that happened in the past. Today, decide to move toward this word – FORGIVENESS.

Let's walk through four powerful truths about forgiveness. First:

FORGIVENESS PROTECTS RELATIONSHIPS AND PROMOTES LOVE.

That's what forgiveness does – it protects the person

you love and it promotes love in them and around them. This is the good and helpful choice that Ephesians is talking about. This is the language that is going to protect, that is going to promote love. We all need people in our lives who do not bring up our mistakes, because we are all sinners.

While teaching one Sunday on *Sticks and Stones*, something happened that hasn't happened to me in 15 years of ministry. Often, before I go on stage to speak, people pray over me. On this particular Sunday, as a couple finished praying for me, the worship team was finishing the last song. I was confident that I had enough time, because all I had to do was get up from the chair I was sitting in and walk onto the stage.

When I stood up from the chair, though, a wire that runs from my mic to the receiver behind my back got caught on the arm of the chair, which then caused the thin microphone on my face to shoot straight back to my ear, rather than pointing toward my mouth. I grabbed the thin mic and tried to move it back toward my mouth, but it did not budge. It is a very fragile piece of technology that our production team has told me not to touch. I am now completely rebelling against those instructions in a panic.

The worship team has stopped playing and a brief video begins setting up the message. (*We play a short video that pertains to the message between the worship and sermon portions of our service.*) I heard the phrase, 'Sticks and Stones will break my bones' from the video, and my heart began to race. The intro video had started and I was still fighting with my mic! Again, I heard the phrase, 'Sticks and Stones will break my bones' and the mic was now sticking straight up in the air. At this point, the band was walking off the stage that I should have been walking onto. One of the band members walked backstage, saw me, and asked, "What are you doing back here? You are supposed to be up there!" (pointing toward the stage).

By now I am feeling helpless just standing there, of course; I point at the mic and he offers to help. What was probably 30 seconds felt like five minutes of him fidgeting as I tried to rush him, letting him know the Sticks and Stones intro was about to end. He was calm and moved slowly and deliberately with the mic. I thought to myself, "I don't want to break your bones, but I need to go!" Two other band members came up to join in the relief effort... Now I have three people working on me right behind the stage I'm supposed to be on and we hear the intro video end. Then ... silence.

Just silence. Now, it all lasted only 38 seconds, but the pause felt like for-ev-er. (*Because we are a society of noise - we cannot deal with two seconds of silence!*) By the time I finally made it out onto the stage, everyone clapped nervously and the awkward silence was over and the message started. Of course, we all got a good laugh out of it. But, to be honest, I didn't want it to be something people brought up over and over again.

The next Sunday rolled around. I expected someone to make a funny comment about it, but no one did. I really expected someone to mock me and say something like, "Now Micah, remember not to get stuck this time!" No one said anything about me being late coming up onto the stage the previous Sunday – except for one person. Well, there is always that one person. Okay, not really, not even that one person said anything mean.

Here is the point: *you* get to decide if you're that one person – it's your choice. I am blessed to be surrounded by a team that uses words that bless, encourage and forgive. Instead of making me feel embarrassed or hold that moment over my head, the team worked together to improve the process to avoid something like that happening again, but never pointed a finger or held it over me.

Bringing up an offense over and over again does not solve anything. Whether it was intentional or unintentional, you can't go back; you can't change it; you can only change how you will move into the future.

We have all messed up and we all need this word – forgiveness.

> **He who covers over an offense promotes love, but whoever repeats the matter separates close friends.** *(Proverbs 17:9)*

With our words, we can cover over an offense. We can choose to not bring up mistakes or we can choose to repeat things that destroy the relationships in our lives. Do you believe you can say things that would damage the relationships in your life? Of course. Or you can promote love with your words. Do you believe that? Do you believe you can say things that move a relationship past the hurt and pain? You can actually say things that promote love.

We have already talked about serving up positive words. We have already talked about our words being like a hammer – building up or tearing down. Now let's go back to the idea that our words are like a shovel.

Let this sink in: our words are like a shovel.

You choose: dig up or cover over.

In Alberta, Canada, a 39-year-old Canadian decided to add a room onto his house. He wanted to dig the footers himself – one of his friends told him he should wait for the city to mark where any underground lines were. He didn't think that was very important; he figured it was no big deal where any power lines or gas lines were in the yard. Well, on the second day of digging, you guessed it, he hit a natural gas line. He didn't just hit it, he ruptured it. According to the Alberta newspaper, the man had just enough time to get away from his house before the whole thing exploded. And the explosion was so powerful, it knocked him down. What caused the explosion? He was digging.

Do you know something that you could dig up from the past that would cause an explosion in your relationship?

If I dig something up from the past and send it over to you, you will explode. When you explode, the heat's off of me. Even though the heat is off of me, I've just blown up my relationship.

There are explosions happening every day in relationships because our words are digging instead of covering. Proverbs 17:9 says we need to promote love – we need to cover over an offense - the Hebrew word translated *cover over* is:

הסכ *which means to cover, protect, overwhelm* – in other words, I am going to cover over this situation with forgiveness.

To *cover over* does not mean to ignore it, deny it hurt or pretend it didn't happen. On the contrary, it means to acknowledge it, directly deal with it but then through forgiveness bury it to insure it never "comes up" again as a weapon against the other person.

When someone wrongs you, you have to decide if you are going to repeat the offense at every opportunity, or if you are going to protect your relationship and forgive, not saying anything else about it once it has been forgiven. You have to make this decision. I choose, I am going to protect this relationship by covering up this offense. To promote love, we are going to move forward. We are going to have a great and strong relationship because we both choose forgiveness.

Here is the second powerful truth about forgiveness:

FORGIVENESS KEEPS NO RECORD OF ANY MISTAKES.
Love doesn't keep a ledger – it doesn't store your

wrongs. If you want a relationship to work, you have to allow a reset. **Forgiveness is a reset.** If you don't have that, then the relationship is doomed for failure. No matter how special a relationship is, it can be ruined by unforgiveness. it is doomed for failure if there is no forgiveness.

Can you imagine if I didn't forgive my kids? What if every time I see my kids, I remind them of their failures in life? How awesome would my home be? They come out for breakfast in the morning, and I say something like, "Hey, do you remember the time you forgot your homework ... struck out in that baseball game... broke the light ... messed up the recipe ... lost the game ... forgot your lines ... disobeyed ... had a bad attitude ... didn't respect me, and got grounded ...?" Wouldn't that be awkward? The relationship with my kids would be doomed.

If we keep records of all the mistakes in our relationships, those relationships will fail because there is nothing to build on when all we do is remind the other person of the past.

A relationship cannot survive without forgiveness. At some point, you need it, just like water. And when you don't have it, the relationship can't move forward.

Start each day fresh. Every day is a clean slate. Forgiveness is a choice to live in the present, letting go of the past and forgiving. We have to make the choice to not keep a record of wrongs, and instead, to cover over the offense.

Love decides, "I love this person so much that I am going to cover their offense."

> ***"Love keeps no record of being wronged."***
> (1 Corinthians 13:5)

Those six words, "keeps no record of being wronged," are just one Greek word:

λογίζομαι *which means to keep record, to enter into a ledger, to calculate.*

In other words, when I choose to forgive, I remove your debt to me. From that point on, when I see you, I am not going to take what you did into account. I am not going to calculate how to get even. Love doesn't pull out a calculator and add up all the hurt from all the years. Have you ever pulled out your emotional calculator when you're in conflict with someone? It's easy to do. First, you bring up the past wrong, then add in how badly it affected you at the time because of how you were already feeling, multiply it by how many years it's been festering in you. If you are an emotional calculator, your relationship is doomed. If you calculate, then words kill. Because unforgiveness is a poison inside of you and all it leads to is bitterness, rage, harsh words, anger, and slander. Because I can't let go; I can't forgive you; this relationship will implode.

Jesus tells us to choose forgiveness when people wrong us. This is how the conversation goes:

> *Then Peter came to Jesus and asked, "Lord, how often should I forgive someone who sins against me? Seven times?" "No, not seven times," Jesus replied, "but seventy times seven!"*
> *(Matthew 18:21-22)*

70 x 7! Wow! Peter was trying to impress Jesus with the number 7. Peter asked if that was good to forgive someone 7 times. Jesus's response is HUGE! 70x 7. That is a big number. For mathematicians reading this, you have already done the calculation: 490 times. Hold on, *Jesus wasn't teaching multiplication, He was teaching forgiveness.* The number is meant to illustrate the grace God gives to us and also the supernatural ability God gives to us to be forgiving people. He wants us to give what God has given to us: an endless supply of forgiveness.

You may be pushing back, asking, "you want ME to forgive?" Let me answer clearly: YES! God is calling you to forgive. If you don't know if you can do it, I understand, it's tough. But you really can. It doesn't mean you instantly establish a relationship again or even ever completely restore the relationship. It definitely doesn't mean you forget what happened. Forgiveness does mean you don't calculate it against them and you don't dig up the offense during an argument.

I know that you can forgive, because you most likely forgive every day ... Do you have pets? If yes, then you practice forgiveness every day! Pet owners have to be some of the most forgiving people in the world. You are very forgiving of animals, time and time again, because pets are always doing things that drive you crazy!

I think we are better at forgiveness of animals than humans. Pets destroy pillows and leave stuffing every-where, they tear holes in furniture, they dig through the trash and drag it all over the house, they dig holes in the yard. After all of these offenses, we still keep them around!

You might take a dog's treats away, or make him sleep

in the backyard, or – no – in the laundry room (because the backyard is too cold and scary!).

Quick question: what if your kids made the mess your dog makes? They would be sleeping in the backyard for a week!

Yep, we are better at forgiving animals than forgiving humans. We've got to be nicer to people than we are to our pets!

Love covers over offenses. Love keeps no record of mistakes. Love is something that's driven by this word: forgiveness. Definitely continue to be nice to your pets, but share that love and that level of forgiveness with the people in your life also.

Where do we need to start? Start with Jesus.

Jesus taught us to forgive 70 x 7. He didn't just teach us the concept of forgiveness, he also showed us what that looks like by offering that forgiveness to us. Jesus does not want to condemn you; Jesus is not mad at you. Jesus wants to forgive you. Jesus doesn't want to dig up your past; He wants to cover your past in His blood. He wants to help protect your relationship with God and overwhelm you with an amazing, lifechanging love.

From the cross, Jesus cried out, "Father forgive them." And we think that He was talking to the Roman soldiers who nailed His hands to the cross, and He was. But He was also looking through time, through all eternity, and He looked at you. He looked at everything you have ever done, everything you have ever said, and all the hurt you have ever caused. Think about it, all of your regrets and sin were placed on Him at that moment on the cross. He was speaking to the pain you caused Him as He suffered on that cursed tree as a sacrifice for you: "Forgive them."

Jesus loves you and keeps no record of your wrongs. When you come to Him, He doesn't reject you or take revenge – He takes you in. He is not mad at you; He is madly in love with you. His forgiveness is absolutely amazing! He wants to cover your past in His blood.

He's not going to dig up your past. He's going to use His words, not to tear you down, but to build you back up.

When you begin a relationship with Jesus, protect this relationship. Your daily connection with Jesus is where the power for you to be an agent of forgiveness comes from. When you remember what Jesus did on the cross, you will live a blessed life.

> **Blessed is the man whose sin the Lord will never count against him.** (Romans 4:8)

Another word for blessed is happy. You will be happy when you receive God's mercy and when you give it away.

Here is the third powerful truth about forgiveness:

FORGIVENESS STARTS WITH MY RELATIONSHIP WITH GOD

Before you try to forgive someone else, start by receiving mercy from God. A clean slate, and a new beginning in that mercy is amazing. When I know true forgiveness from God, then I am able to forgive others also. We think that God is a God of justice - He is, but He poured out his justice on the cross and Jesus took our punishment and our place. Jesus got beat up on the cross so we don't have to beat up ourselves.

When you ask God to forgive you, all of a sudden, you receive mercy instead of justice. You need to start your relationship with God and keep that relationship tight. Because the beautiful thing is that when you wake up in the morning and you greet God, or when you haven't been to church in awhile and come back on Sunday, He doesn't ask where you've been. He doesn't remind you of what you did yesterday, or last week. He doesn't say, "It's about time you served me!" The Bible says His mercies and compassions are new every morning; great is His faithfulness. Our amazing God offers a clean slate. His mercy is amazing.

It's like a story I heard about this woman whose daughter was getting married. The bride was a bit of a 'bride-zilla,' but the mom was even worse, directing everyone everywhere and complaining about everything. She hassled the photographer throughout the evening of the wedding. After a few weeks, the time came when they got all the pictures back. When they looked at the photos, the mom complained to the photographer only about the pictures that she, herself, was in, and told him, "These pictures of me don't do me justice!" The photographer replied, "Ma'am, you don't need justice, you need mercy!"

Because of what Christ did on the Cross, we don't get justice, we get *mercy*.

Merciful words come from the heart that has received God's mercy. It's a lot easier to criticize than it is to sympathize, until we realize that the person who has hurt us is in need of the same mercy we have received from God. When we choose to share mercy, this actually brings good things into our lives.

> *The merciful man does himself good, but the cruel man does himself harm.* (Proverbs 11:17)

You ought to be merciful simply because it makes you happy. It's a boomerang blessing: what you give is what you get.

I was recently reminded of the story about Tex Watson. He's a guy who brutally murdered seven people. Seven! They were totally random, horrible acts. Once Tex was condemned to multiple life sentences, he had a chaplain come visit him in prison. He heard about God's mercy and forgiveness. Tex claims at that moment, even though he knew he didn't derserve it, he became a believer and received forgiveness. Years after this jailhouse conversion, a woman visited his cell. He rarely took visitors. The lady asked him three very simple questons: Had he really changed? Was his conversion really legit? Was he really sorry?

They visited for a long time and after an hour the woman looked him in the eye and said, "I forgive you." As the woman stood to leave, she told Tex that she was the daughter of two of the people he had murdered: John and Lydia Limbanks. She had just spent an hour with the man who had killed her parents and felt free of any grudges or negativity.

Compare her choice to Sharon Tate's mother. Sharon Tate was another one Tex killed. Sharon's mother refused to forgive. She often expressed her hatred and resentment toward Tex. She allowed bitterness to eat her alive. Literally. In just a few years, she died young. All those close to her described her as a bitter, angry woman.

Don't get me wrong; Tex Watson was not a wonderful man. He deserves to be in prison for the rest of his life. He has even said in interviews that he deserves to be put to death for his choices.

This is the point: the prisoner we set free when we are merciful is ourselves.

The words of Jesus have nothing to do with the justice that is needed for those who make evil decisions. Personally, it is essential that we are merciful. When we are not merciful, we exchange blessings for bitterness. Let's not do that – time is too short and words are too precious.

> **INSTEAD be kind and compassionate to one another, forgiving each other, just as in Christ, God forgave you.** (Ephesians 4:32 NIV)

Instead of all that faultfinding stuff in verse 31 of Ephesians, all of that bitterness, rage, anger, harsh words, slander – which is all poison – choose forgiveness. Will you choose to show mercy? Will you choose to sympathize? Will you choose to be kind? Will you choose to have compassion?

How are you going to forgive? *Just as in Christ, God forgave you.* This leads us to the last powerful truth about forgiveness:

I FORGIVE BECAUSE I AM FORGIVEN

As we end this chapter, there are two big questions for you to consider. First question: Will you ask God for forgiveness? I promise you, if you ask for it, you will receive it. God is not mad at you. He has intentionally put you in the place where you are reading these words, in this moment, so you can connect with his love and mercy, so you can receive this good, helpful and lifechanging news: **He wants to forgive you and you can forgive yourself.**

Before you wrestle with the choice to forgive others, know God's forgiveness personally. Know that you are saved by grace through faith, not by works. Choose to receive the free gift of forgiveness. Whatever you've done, wherever you've been, no matter how much you think you've blown it, no matter how many mistakes you think you have made, God can forgive you. He doesn't have a calculator out. He put all your debt on Jesus and now your debt is zero.

Second question: have you forgiven all the people in your life who have hurt you? Unforgiveness kills relationships. Several years ago, an article in *US News and World Report* claimed that if there is anything in your marriage that you have not forgiven, you actually have a 90% chance of getting a divorce. What is that one thing that you have not forgiven your spouse for? Your friend for? Your parents for? Your worst enemy for?

To give forgiveness, you have to let go and give it to God. You choose: you're not going to let that thing hurt you anymore, and you're going to forgive. I will make you a promise: God will never ask you to forgive someone more than He has forgiven you.

Forgiving others begins with allowing God to forgive you. Once you experience God's forgiveness, you can't help but give away the forgiveness you have received. When your debt is cleared; you should be inspired to clear other's debts to you.

There are three powerful words that bring life and hope to every relationship. We can say these words because Jesus says them to us: *I forgive you.*

PRAYER:

Lord, I ask for forgiveness today. I know that you have brought me to this moment so that I can connect to you and receive this free gift. Through grace and faith I am saved, not by works. I know that no matter what I've done or where I've been, you will not calculate my mistakes. You put all my debt on Jesus, and now my debt is zero. Thank you for your forgiveness, Lord. Jesus, thank you for dying on the cross for me. Jesus, I ask for your help in forgiving others. Help me to let go of the hurts I have been holding onto. I am not going to dig up the past anymore, but rather promote love. No longer will I tear down, but I will build up! Thank you for your example and thank you for changing my heart and changing my relationships. Thank you for forgiving me and thank you for helping me forgive others. Thank you that your mercies and compassions are new every morning. In Jesus' name, Amen.

"

We will speak the
truth *in* **love**.

"

(Ephesians 4:15)

6

YOU CAN HANDLE THE TRUTH

We have talked about five types of words that will change every relationship in your life: words that are positive, words that are Gospel (which simply means Good News), words that heal, compliments, and, perhaps the most needed word, forgiveness. Now it's time to talk about the importance of truth.

In the movie, A Few Good Men, there is a famous trial scene where the two main characters – one played by Tom Cruise and one by Jack Nicholson – are locked in a verbal battle to find out what really happened on a certain fateful night in Guantánamo Bay.

Cruise's character appeals to the hardened colonel and declares, "I want the truth!" building to that infamous line yelled by the colonel, "You can't handle the truth!"

It makes for great drama and sells movie tickets, but it

isn't an accurate statement. We are designed to share and receive truth.

READ TRUTH

For you are God, O Sovereign LORD.
Your words are truth. (2 Samuel 7:28)

When you pause each day to read the Bible, you are allowing truth to enter your heart. Since the overflow of the heart is what your mouth speaks, exposing your heart to truth is essential to speaking truth. Reading, studying and meditating on Scripture is the only way to battle the lies that fill the music, movies and messaging of the world. The journey to becoming a truthful person begins with reading God's Word.

FOLLOW TRUTH

"Teacher," they said, "we know that you are a man of integrity and that you teach the way of God in accordance with the truth. You aren't swayed by others, because you pay no attention to who they are. (Matthew 22:16)

Before you can speak the truth, you have to follow the truth. Who you follow and focus on becomes the main subject and influencer of your conversations. Notice two words in this verse. The word "integrity" and the word "truth." They go together. A person of integrity is going to tell the truth no matter what. Jesus is our example. The people speaking to him in this verse were actually his enemies. Even people who opposed Jesus acknowledged his integrity and his lack of concern for the opinion of others. In John 14:6, Jesus said He is the truth. Follow Jesus.

APPLY TRUTH

> ***Don't just listen to God's Word.***
> ***You must do what it says.*** *(James 1:22)*

When we decide to read God's Word and follow Jesus, we begin to realize we were designed to run on truth. However, the power of truth is found when we actually apply it to our lives and our relationships.

I received this email from a woman who began attending our church during this *Sticks and Stones* series:

Hello! I wanted to let you know I have been coming to church for several weeks now. Before, when I would go to a church, I would not want to return and actually I have always dreaded going to church, but this time with Real Life it's different. I have been back every Sunday and I look forward to it all week long. Our children even look forward to coming and learning. My husband has been going with me and he also looks forward to it and our relationship has grown stronger with your series on the power of words. **We have been applying what we've learned** *into our daily lives and you know what? It's AWESOME!!!!*

Did you catch the key phrase? *We have been applying what we have been learning.* If you apply what you will learn about truth in this chapter to your life, it will have the same results – it will be awesome!

> **Truthful words stand the test of time, but lies are soon exposed.** *(Proverbs 12:19)*

CHOOSE TRUTH

Truth protects and keeps us safe. Truth keeps us grounded. Truth is a light that shines on the path of life. We need truth, and the foundation of relationships is telling the truth. On the contrary, lies create spiritual strongholds in our lives, ruin relationships and eventually destroy our own reputations.

You may not remember a lot of things from this book next month or next year – but I do hope you will remember the key verse of the book:

> **Words kill, words give life;
> they are either poison or fruit – you choose.**
> *(Proverbs 18:21 MSG)*

Every day, every hour, every minute of your life – you are going to choose your words. I pray you will choose words that are positive, not negative; Gospel, not gossip; helpful, not hurtful; compliments, not complaints; and forgiving not fault-finding ...

After today, I pray that you will also speak truth, not lies.

LIES

Lies are everywhere. I want you to think about the words that you have used in your life:

How often do you lie?

Do you have to teach your kids how to lie? No. Why? Because it comes naturally, doesn't it? It's part of our sinful nature.

Lies can really fall into a couple of different categories.

First Category:

Occasionally. Usually stretching the truth. You tell somebody you were on the football team in high school, when you know you were really the water-boy. You occasionally lie because you don't want to hurt someone's feelings, so you lie a little bit about something. A friend approaches you, and you notice they recently got a haircut and you hate it. What do you do when they ask you what you think? You lie of course! The other occasional lie is the Pinocchio lie. Those lies that help enhance your story; the fish was 'this' big, when really it was 'this' tiny. So, while you are reading this, go ahead and nod your head to yourself if you would say, "Oh, yeah – I lie occasionally."

Second Category:

Often. Here are a few examples of how often people lie:

We lie about our finances – we look like we are okay, but we are not. We so often spend all of our money to keep up with the Joneses, when the Joneses are beyond broke themselves trying to stay ahead of us! We spend money we don't have to buy things we don't need, to impress people we don't like.

Living beyond your means is a lie. Our competitive nature gets us in trouble because other people live in a big house and have a luxury car, so we feel we need to have those same things as well. We don't take into account that they have been saving up for that house for 15 years and have been working at a job for 20 years to be able to afford those things.

We lie about other people so we can look better. If we can't keep up with someone else, we cut them down. Instead of celebrating another person's success or accomplishments, we often spread lies or rumors to make us feel better or look better.

We tell lies at work to help ourselves get ahead. We stretch the truth on our resumes or exaggerate how many hours a certain project took. We offer up an idea to the boss that our co-worker mentioned to us, and we take the credit.

We sometimes lie for no reason; "I don't know why I just said that mean thing about my friend, I don't really feel that way, it just came out!" We tell someone we have been on a cruise ship, even though our only boating experience was a float at a water park.

Care to admit you lie often?

Ready for the one that scares me the most?!

THE TRUTH ABOUT LIES

So, you may be saying, "I am glad I am not in the second category – I only tell an 'occasional' lie ..." But let this sink in: **a lie is a lie**.

Notice what this verse says about lying:

> *The LORD detests lying lips, but He delights in people who are trustworthy. (Proverbs 12:22 NIV)*

Lying seems to be a way of life for many people. We lie at the drop of a hat. The book The Day America Told

the Truth says that:
- 91% of those surveyed lie routinely about matters they consider trivial
- 36% lie about important matters
- 86% of kids lie regularly to parents
- 75% of Americans lie to friends
- 69% of married couples lie to their spouses

God doesn't want us to lie – why do we?

LIES ARE REALLY SAYING, "PLEASE LIKE ME"

One of the big reasons we lie is so people will like us, don't you think? We exaggerate the facts, we twist the truth, and we leave out the stuff that doesn't make us look good. We lie about ourselves to make us look better than someone else. And we also lie about somebody else to make people like us better. Lies are trying to manipulate circumstances so people will like the most important person in my life - me.

This is the biggest downside to social media. It may not feel exactly like lying, but we so often are posting just the highlight reel of our lives to show off to the world how amazing we are. We fail to post the hardships and the struggles, or even just the boring weeks of our lives. We may tell ourselves, 'well, who wants to see the boring parts of my life?' But, really, we don't want anyone to know that our life may be monotonous 26 days of each month when we're just struggling to pay the bills. Instead, we'll show them the highlight of the four days of the month when we're splurging all of the remaining money from our paycheck! But we look good on those four days, don't we?

LIES ARE SELFISH

They really are. I am using my words for *me* – for *my* benefit, for *my* reputation, for *my* protection, for *my* promotion. Here is the reality:

> ***A lying tongue hates those it hurts, and***
> ***a flattering mouth works ruin.***
> *(Proverbs 26:28)*

There was an article in *People* magazine about 20 years ago illustrating what lies can do. Bob Harris was fired as meteorologist for both the *New York Times* and WCBS radio in New York. After 10 years as a professional weatherman, Harris had been caught in a serious lie. He had never earned the doctorate in geophysics from Columbia University that he had claimed. In fact, he had nothing but a high school diploma.

People ✔ @people · 14h ⌄
Weatherman Bob Harris was only off one degree, but the mistake nearly cost him his career.

"I was so ashamed," says Harris, 39. "I was publicly disgraced. I went from $75,000 a year to zip. I had lost everything." He admits it was a dreadful mistake on his part and feels it played a role in his divorce. *"I took a shortcut that turned out to be the long way around, and one day the bill came due. I will be sorry as long as I am alive."*

LIES LEAVE US EMPTY

Lies are only a temporary fix that may make us feel good for a moment, but a lie only adds another level to a house of cards. Even if lies temporarily make us feel good or momentarily cover up a truth we try to avoid, they leave an empty feeling because deep down inside we are disappointing ourselves and, even more importantly, we are disappointing our Creator. God didn't design us to run on lies and that is why He hates them so much:

> **The LORD detests lying lips, but He delights in people who are trustworthy.** *(Proverbs 12:22 NIV)*

What does the word detest mean?

Detest comes from the Hebrew word **הָ בַ עוֹת** which means disgusting, abomination, to make nauseous.

That is what lying does to God. If you have as much

trouble spelling nauseous as I do, maybe a better description is 'throw-up.'

If you are a parent, how many times have you had to clean up your kids' throw-up? Have you noticed that before they throw up, they have to eat something that is totally gross coming back up? They can't just drink clear Gatorade or chicken broth – they have to drink purple Kool-Aid and eat hamburger helper, right?

Are you a sympathy puker? Do you feel like throwing up when you see someone else throw up? Are you getting sick to your stomach just from reading the last couple of paragraphs?

There was one time when our kids were all very young and I was out of town overnight. My wife, Lori, and the kids had had a rough day, so Lori ordered pizza to make life easier. They all ate the pizza, but then, everybody started getting tired and fussy. They all started crying. Lori and I were talking about this recently; it was the only time that everyone in the house was crying at the same time! She got everyone to bed, but it wasn't long before one of them called her to say they didn't feel good. She soothed one child, just in time to hear another precious child lean over their bed and throw up from three feet off the ground. It fell onto a hardwood floor. Processed peperoni and cheese hit the floor and slid everywhere – all over the bed, all over the room, even under the closet door. Ever had one of those days?

When we lie, it makes God nauseous. Like eating bad pizza. God basically says that when people lie, it makes him want to puke.

So, the next time a lie is about to come out of your mouth and you think, "It's no big deal; everybody does it," Remember this:

God hates it. It makes him sick.

Why does God hate lying so much? Well, let's look a little deeper.

Where do lies come from? Where do they originate?

> **There is no truth in him. When the devil lies, he speaks his native language, for he is a liar and the father of lies.** (John 8:44)

What is Satan's strategy? He wants to use lies to take us from the truth of who Jesus is. He doesn't want us to Read God's Word or follow God's Son. The root of all lies is **the lies that Satan tells us**:

- Get more stuff and be happy.

- Look a certain way and everyone will like you.
- Look out for number 1 – you are number 1.
- Please everybody.
- Worry about everything.
- God doesn't want you to have fun.
- The only way you will be happy is to NOT follow Jesus.

... the lies get darker and more depressing ...

- You will never amount to anything.
- You have nothing to look forward to.
- You are not going to make it through this.
- You have messed up too much for God to love you.
- You have gone too far for God to use you.
- You will never change.

Have you ever heard those lies before? Sure you have. The devil is crafty but he is not creative. Those lies are powerful because many of us believe them. They are so easy to believe, aren't they? That's why Satan continues to use them – because he knows how easily we can be distracted from the truth and he knows how powerful these lies are. Each lie takes us further and further away from our source ... from the truth ... from God.

Now let's look at the alternative to lies: speaking truth.

*Jesus, the Anointed One, unveils truth wrapped
in tender mercy. (John 1:17 The Passion)*

TRUTH

God delights in someone who is truthful: truth - full.
Full of truth.

Now this is very important; you don't want you to
miss this. You need to speak the truth – not lies! Some
people think that this means as long as you say "I'll tell
you what's on my mind," that this counts as speaking
the truth. No – speaking the truth is not the same as
speaking your mind.

- I'll tell you the truth – I think you are ugly.
- I'll tell you the truth – I don't like being married to
  you.
- I'll tell you the truth – I don't feel like going to
  church today.
- I'll tell you the truth – I hate my boss.
- I'll tell you the truth – my parents are dumb.

That is NOT speaking truth.

God delights in people who are truthful. God does
not delight in people who are not afraid to speak their
minds, share their opinions or preferences, people who
can share their feelings at the exact moment they feel

something. Feelings are very deceptive. Just because you feel something in a moment, it doesn't mean that it's a truth. Satan often uses our feelings to trip us up. God is the only one who can tell us if something is really true.

Among the most popular messages of our society today is the proclamation, "Follow your heart!" The culture has conditioned us to place a very high value on our own desires and emotions. In fact, we are encouraged to base both our major life decisions and our daily lifestyle choices upon how we feel. This trickles down into our conversations and our culture advises us to always say or do what we feel at the moment.

For example, when we argue with people that we love, we should be very cautious about saying what we feel like saying in that moment.

A married couple came in to my office for some help. The past weekend they had been in an argument and their emotions and anger elevated with each comment. Each one was so eager to win the argument that they went too far with their words. They got out their verbal hammers and shovels. They tore each other down and dug up the past. It felt right at the moment, but they were sitting in my office because they said what they felt at the moment: "I hate you" and then even worse, "I wish I'd never met you!"

> *A rebel shouts in anger;*
> *a wise man holds his temper in and cools it.*
> (*Proverbs 29:22 LB*)

It may feel like truth at the moment, but when we pause and think about it, it isn't truth all. Feelings are not truth, even though the culture tells you, "Listen to your heart! Do or say what feels right to you." Don't believe this advice even though it permeates everything from love songs to children's movies. God gives us a completely different heart and emotions:

> *"He who trusts in his own heart is a fool" and*
> *"The heart is deceitful above all things."*
> (*Jeremiah 17:9*)

Truth goes beyond feelings. Truth is motivated by love. We should speak the truth in love. Like Jesus, we should make sure our truth is wrapped in mercy. The Bible challenges us to be people who are "truthful."

People who are truth - full:

TRUST GOD
When I lie, I am basically saying, "I can't trust God – I am

going to go out on my own and make my own story."

Speaking truth is saying words that are powerful and that shatter the lies that the world is telling you.

The truth is you can trust God and He can change you. Earlier in this chapter, I pointed out that lies make God nauseous. But this is important: Lies don't make Him want to throw up because He is sick of you messing up – lies make Him sick because He has so much more for you. More plans for you. More to give you. More to show you. He hates watching lies hold you back from your best life.

Remember where it started, all the way back in the book of Genesis when Adam and Eve were in the garden. The devil told them they could be like God – lying to them. He also wants you to believe the lie, so that in turn - you start telling lies. And then, just like Adam and Eve discovered, one lie leads to separation from God, then one lie leads to another, which then leads to further separation from God. Which ultimately leads to where the devil wants you to end up – where you are living a lie. We claim one thing; secretly we are something entirely different.

Satan is the liar – Jesus is the truth.

Start a new habit today: Speak truth.

Truth sets you free and brings life to everyone around you.

For every lie, there is a truth. And the Bible lays out the truth for us to hold onto.

LIE: worry about everything.
TRUTH: **Trust in the LORD with all your heart.**
(Proverbs 3:5a)

LIE: you will never amount to anything, you will never change.
TRUTH: **For we are God's masterpiece. He has created us anew in Christ Jesus, so we can do the good things he planned for us long ago.** *(Ephesians 2:10 NLT)*

LIE: You don't have anything to look forward to.
TRUTH: **"For I know the plans I have for you," declares the LORD, "plans to prosper you and not to harm you, plans to give you hope and a future."** *(Jeremiah 29:11)*

LIE: You can't do it.
TRUTH: **I can do all things through Christ who strengthens me.** *(Philippians 4:13 NKJV)*

LIE: You are not going to make it through this. Instead, know this:
TRUTH: **We are more than conquerors through him who loved us.** *(Romans 8:37)*

DOUBLE LIE: You have messed up too much for God to love you. You have gone too far for God to use you.
*TRUTH: **If we confess our sins, He is faithful and just and will forgive us.*** (1 John 1:9a)

GOD CAN CHANGE ME

Once, there was a pastor in Oklahoma who had built a house of lies for so many years, no one realized it until his entire life came crashing down around him. For him, it started at a young age. He bought into the lie that he was number one. The lie often sounds like: "Look out for number one and do what feels good to you."

In the 4th grade, he became addicted to pornography with a magazine he found under his dad's bed. He went to college, got into the ministry, got married and had kids, all the while hiding this addiction. He had to lie to everyone to maintain an appearance. He eventually had an affair.

He finally came clean with both his wife and with his church.

He then resigned the ministry and worked in a lumber yard for 18 months.

At 5:30 every morning – he read out loud the truths

above that you just read. Somewhere in the middle of those 18 months, as he would speak them out loud to himself, he started to actually believe them in his heart. He saw God make changes in his life. After some more time, some intentional healing and accountability: he is back in ministry! His wife and family all love and admire him. Are you ready for this? He is on staff at a church ministering to more than 10,000 people every weekend!

Speak truth – not lies.

> **Jesus said, "If you hold to my teaching, you are really my disciples. Then you will know the truth, and the truth will set you free."**
> *(John 8:31-32)*

Now what I don't want to happen is for all of us to admit we are a bunch of liars, try to work on it, and we do good from Sunday to about Wednesday, but give up or forget why we are even doing it. I want God to change us and truly, genuinely set us free.

This isn't just about our freedom. You see, when the truth sets us free, we can help each other become free as well. I can speak truth much easier when I am applying truth to my own life. I can speak truth in love much more effectively if I have decided to love and follow Jesus myself.

If I love you, I am going to tell you the truth.
If you are standing in the street and a truck is speeding down the road, I am going to tell at you, "Get out of the street!" I am not telling you to get out of the street because I am judging your decision to be in the street. I am not telling you to get out of the street because I am trying to control your life and tell you where you can or can't stand. I am not telling you to get out of the street because I think I am a better person because I am on the sidewalk. I am telling you to get out of the street because I LOVE YOU AND WANT YOU TO LIVE!

Love should motivate my words and sometimes the hard truth is just what a person needs to bring healing and help to them. I love you enough to tell you, "Hey, you are in the street and if you stay there, that truck is going to injure you and may kill you. Love motivates me to tell you the truth about what needs to change in your life. Sometimes the most loving thing you can do is tell someone they are going the wrong way, doing the wrong thing, need to stop a certain pattern.

Let me be honest, this has been a struggle for me. I wanted the person to like me more than loving them enough to tell them the truth. I have had to learn that if I genuinely love someone, the short term pain of telling them the truth is worth their temporary rejection of me as they process that truth. You see, I have discovered that even though the person hearing the truth may reject it, project their rebellion back on me, or be too prideful to receive it, I still need to say it: Even if they stay in the street, telling that person you care about the truth in the right way is always the most loving thing we can do. When truth is shared in love there is potential for healing.

> *The tongue that brings healing is a tree of life,*
> *but a deceitful tongue crushes the spirit.*
> (*Proverbs. 15:4*)

> *Truthful lips endure forever, but a lying*
> *tongue lasts only a moment.*
> (*Proverbs 12:19*)

BEFORE I TELL YOU THE TRUTH, I NEED TO BE HONEST WITH MYSELF

Let me be real here, right now. I have found that when I lie, I lie because I don't truly trust God. I believe my lie will work better than the truth. I want people to like me, but I've realized that you can't have relationships built on lies. I want to look good but lies are ugly.

You may be saying, "Why am I reading this book? And why this chapter?" I'll tell you why. Because the Holy Spirit is starting to show you what needs to change. Maybe your parents have no idea what you are doing. Maybe you are struggling with telling others the truth because there are lies in your own life. Maybe you have an emotional affair going on. Whatever the deception, you know you have to deal with it. You must get free from it because you were not designed run on the fuel of lies.

How can you be set free?

There are two things I want you to do today.

1) Confess and receive God's forgiveness.

This has to be where we start – getting honest with God and allowing Him to forgive us.

> *If we confess our sins, He is faithful and just*
> *and will forgive us our sins and purify us*
> *from all unrighteousness. (1 John 1:9)*

Can God really forgive me even I have been living a lie?

I want you to have a real life, present day, moment of truth story. Jesus wants to set you free today, so follow along.

Step one – confess to God.
I know God has forgiven me, but something is still not right.

2) Confess to the appropriate people so we can be healed.

If you really want to be free, you have to take this second step.

> *Therefore confess your sins to each other and*
> *pray for each other so that you may be healed.*
> (James 5:16a)

Note: this is not so that we may be forgiven; it is so that we may be healed.

You need to confess to the appropriate people.

Who are the appropriate people?

Let me tell you, without exception, it depends.

Not everyone needs to know everything. For some things, it is better that only a few people know.
Honesty - everything you say is true, but everything that is true doesn't need to be said.

Some people think honesty means I have to tell everybody everything. No. Let me give you an example.
I hear things that people say about me that are lies.

There are entire websites dedicated to lies about me.

A year ago a lady told me, "I have told and written hundreds of lies about you." Here is the problem with that confession – it didn't help me. I haven't seen her since. Who should she have confessed to? I could think of hundreds of other people that would have been good to start with.

If you confess to someone who is involved in your life, here is a good question to guide you:

Could the short-term pain caused by your confession lead to deeper intimacy? This lady that tells me she has spread gossip about me - we aren't going to be friends; she doesn't even go to my church.

If you have a secret that involves your spouse, know that when you confess it to them, it could lead to deeper intimacy and healing, then that is a confession you need to make. (*Side note: if your confessed secret will cause tremendous emotional pain to your spouse or close family member, please reach out to your pastor and even a certified Christian counselor BEFORE you schedule this confession. Seek wise counsel from spiritual authority you trust and even professional counselors to navigate this necessary but difficult step*).

You may be saying, "Oh, I don't want to do it."

Maybe your struggle is what my struggle was - that you really don't trust God. You believe your lie will work better than the truth. Is that you?

At Real Life, we encourage people to bring their lies, bring their drugs, their addictions, their imperfections. All are welcome here. We are not going to pretend that we are perfect, that we don't need a Savior to forgive us and that we don't need a God who can set us free. We are not holding anything back in this book – the moment of truth stories just get more real and more powerful.

Today, I encourage you to be real with yourself. Right now, face head on the secrets and the lies that have trapped you. Satan is a liar and there is no freedom in lies. Stop hiding behind the lies. Get real about the fact that you need to confess to God and confess to each other.

> *He who conceals his sins does not prosper,*
> *but whoever confesses and renounces*
> *them finds mercy. (Proverbs 28:13)*

Once we confess, which simply means we tell the truth about ourselves, then we find mercy and freedom. Once we experience mercy and freedom, we can help someone else experience it. We cannot tell someone to get out of the street, if we are standing in the street ourselves. Well, I guess we can but our appeal isn't going to be very motivating. It's like the parent who is holding a cigarette while telling their kid not to smoke. You see, once I move to the sidewalk, then my appeal for you to get out of the street carries much more power and influence. So let's start with us.

We begin to speak the truth when we are truthful with ourselves. We begin to speak the truth in love when we remember that God loves us no matter what. Also, God loves us too much to allow us to stay where we are. When we step into truth and start to live a truthful life, it is like stepping from darkness to light. We begin to walk in truth, speak the truth and love the truth because we were designed to live on truth. The closer you get to truth them more you realize **truth is not a principle; truth is a person.**

> ### *Jesus answered, "I am the way,*
> ### *THE TRUTH, and the life!"*
> *(John 14:6)*

Heavenly Father, I pray that people reading this chapter right now will find mercy today in your presence. And as we close this chapter, show them how to apply it.

If lying is an issue for you – maybe it is occasionally, maybe it is often, maybe you are living a lie. Would you confess this to God right now? Jesus shed his blood on the cross for you, He loves you and He has more for you. The devil is going to try to convince you that you will be better off lying than living according to God's truth.

Pause for a moment and go back to page 168 and read back over the LIES. Identify which LIE you struggle with the most right now. I want to challenge you to memorize the TRUTH that opposes that lie.

Decide right now to belive the truth, to trust Jesus, to follow Jesus, and to walk in truth so that you can speak the truth in love to the people you care about the most.

PRAYER:
Father in heaven, show me what needs to change in me. Thank you that you love me right where I am today. Also, thank you that you love me too much to leave me where I am. Jesus, thank you for dying for me, thank you that you are alive. Fill my life with truth and make me new – I want to follow you. Forgive me for the lies I have told, set me free from the lies I have believed and I commit today to follow your truth and share your truth in love with others.

"

You have said kind and encouraging words to me.

"

(Ruth 2:13)

7

JUST BE NICE

Did you grow up watching Mr. Rogers' Neighborhood? I recently asked that question at our staff retreat and there were people in their 50's all the way down to an intern who was 20 who answered, "Yes." Whether you watched him or not or liked him or not, this guy was on TV for more than 30 years. In fact, Mister Rogers' Neighborhood is one of the longest-running programs in television history, having produced more than 870 episodes. That's almost five times as many as Friends!

Why did so many people tune in? What was it about his show that kept kids and their parents coming back?

There a lot of four letter words out there these days, but we need more of this one – NICE. The guy was nice. **He spoke in a kind, encouraging way to his viewers.**

Guess what? People like people who are nice so they kept watching. The success of this show is how genuine and kind Mr. Rogers was to everyone who tuned in or who turned up on his show.

Why was Mr. Rogers so nice?

Did you watch the recent movie documentary on Fred Rogers? I'd encourage you to do so. It is very insightful. In it, you find out his secret. You see, Mr. Rogers was an ordained minister. He felt called by God to help children. He realized that television was the best platform at that time to get his message out. His secret is found in his favorite number, 143. It is even rumored that Mr. Rogers weighed 143 pounds almost all of his adult life. One episode he explained that "I" has one letter, "love" has four letters and "you" has three letters. 1.4.3.

What caused him to be so NICE (a four-letter word) was another four-letter word: L-O-V-E.

Today I want to talk about a life-changing choice you can make – this choice will change every relationship in your life. This choice will change your marriage, your relationship with your kids, your family, your friends. Making this choice will change your workplace and change social media platforms. This choice is simple but powerful and here it is: **choose to be nice and speak kind words to others.**

Does this mean you have to wear a zipper sweater, have puppets on your hands, and change into slippers when you come home? No. But it does mean you have to love.

Did you know that this whole idea of being nice to your neighbors didn't come from Mr. Rogers? He was a pastor – he knew that the concept actually came from Jesus.

> *The man answered, "'You must love the Lord your God with all your heart, all your soul, all your strength, and all your mind.' And, 'Love your neighbor as yourself.' "Right!" Jesus told him. "Do this and you will live!" The man wanted to justify his actions, so he asked Jesus, "And who is my neighbor?"* (Luke 10:27-29)

Jesus is saying your relationship with God and your relationship with others is actually connected. You can't say that you love God and hate other people. As a matter of fact, how you treat people is a reflection of your relationship with God. If you love God and are close to Him, you are going to love others and be nice to them.

This guy in Luke 10 heard what Jesus said – love God and love others; we know we are supposed to do that, right?

This guy did, too, but wanted to make excuses, so he asks this question – who is my neighbor? His thought behind the question is: I don't want to be nice to everybody!

Jesus answers his question by telling a story, where He demonstrates that loving people and being nice to them is a choice anyone can make. When you love God, you are nice to people.

We know we should talk in a kind way to others, but there are three things getting in the way – three 'Enemies of Nice'. Three things that get in the way of you and me choosing nice, saying nice things and being nice to others.

Let me tell you why I am not nice, and why you are not nice – it's due to one of these three things:

ENEMY #1: SELFISHNESS

Definition of selfishness: concerned excessively about yourself; to concentrate on your own wants without regard for other's needs. Selfishness starts with small things, small decisions, that are hurtful but more subtle. Unchecked selfishness grows and becomes vicious and violent – notice how Jesus starts this story:

> ***A Jewish man was traveling from Jerusalem down to Jericho, and he was attacked by bandits. They stripped him of his clothes, beat him up, and left him half dead beside the road.*** *(Luke 10:30)*

This is full-throttle selfishness. These bandits didn't care about this guy; they took things from him, caused him pain and showed no concern for him. You may say, "Well, I would never steal from somebody else! Stealing is wrong."

How many times do we rob someone's story they are telling because our story is more interesting? You have stolen the spotlight by one-upping their story.

"I jumped out of the way when this bike was coming."

"That's nothing, I jumped out of an airplane."

"Pray for my dad; he has the flu."

"Well, my dad has cancer."

See what I mean?

How many times do we steal someone's self-esteem because we say things that make them feel bad about themselves? How often do we hurt someone and belittle them? When they need love and kind words; instead we give them a verbal beat down? How many times do we ignore the needs of the people in our own house who inside feel like the day has sucked the life out of them and they just need us to stop and pause and say something nice?

These bandits saw this guy for what they could take from him. **When you are always focused on what you want instead of what others need, you will not be nice.** When you see someone for what you can get from them instead of what you need to give to them, selfishness has snuck in.

There is another enemy of choosing nice:

ENEMY #2: BUSY-NESS

Busy-ness is found in the next verse of Luke 10:

> *By chance a priest came along. But when he saw the man lying there, he crossed to the other side of the road and passed him by. (Luke 10:31)*

The people who heard this story knew what was happening. This priest was on his way to work – most of the priests in that day lived in Jericho and went up this road to Jerusalem on their way to work. The crunch of life and the speed of the day did not leave any room for this guy's needs.

Did you know that 60% of Americans admit that the pace of their life is out of control? We have activities that are supposed to help us connect, but they often cause us to disconnect.

The danger of a fast-paced life is when the speed of our day causes us to skim across the relationships that matter most. Instead of pausing to have a conversation and listen, we send a quick text. Instead of sitting down and making sure our message is clear, we send an email and hope for the best. Instead of pausing to say something nice, we fly past the valuable moment on our way to the urgent and immediate task.

But, busy-ness isn't the worst enemy of nice. Not speaking nice words over time leads to:

ENEMY #3: NO EMPATHY

This is the most deadly enemy to marriages and friendships. Empathy is the ability to understand and share the feelings of another person. When there is no empathy, that relationship – whatever that relationship is – is in jeopardy.

No empathy is much more dangerous than busy-ness. You see, when I am too busy, I am going too fast to notice the need or say the nice thing. However, when I have no empathy, I am not too busy; I see their need, I know they are hurting, but I refuse to take the time to think about how it feels to be them – in their shoes.

Empathy is the ability to feel what someone else feels. No empathy disconnects all my compassion and I am able to look at their need without any loving response. Notice the lack of empathy in the next verse:

> *A Temple assistant walked over and looked at him lying there, but he also passed by on the other side.* (Luke 10:32)

Now that we have seen the enemies of nice, let's look at an example of being nice from the same passage.

NICE 101.

> *Then a despised Samaritan came along, and when he saw the man, he felt compassion for him.* (Luke 10:33)

This is a powerful turn in the story because Samaritans were hated and despised. Notice Jesus even says it by calling the man, "a despised Samaritan."

How much were they hated? Well, more than half of the population of Israel was in the northern part known as Galilee, and in-between them was the territory known as Samaria. Samaria was filled with people whose ancestors had intermarried with other nations (not them, but people generations before). So Samaritans are part Jewish and part something else.

Super-religious people known as Pharisees would not even travel through that region. They would cross over the Jordan River and cross back over the Jordan when they got past them. Guess who did NOT take this route? Jesus. He didn't avoid any type of person. He

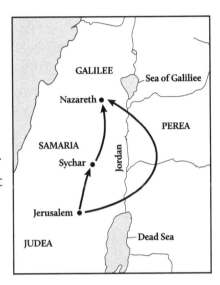

was even nice to a Samaritan woman. His kind words helped her find hope and changed her whole village. Jesus taught us by his life that being nice is a choice.

Nice 101 starts with this:

1. Look beyond differences and love from the heart.

Are people different than you? Yes, but it's the heart that matters. Choose to have compassion on them no matter how different they are from you. The Samaritan in this story, the type of person that Jews actually avoid, has compassion for a Jewish man.

Back in that day, people identified themselves with what they wore (much like gangs or groups today have a certain dress code or colors that distinguish them, styles to stick to). In those days, you could easily identify a Jewish person from a Samaritan just by their clothing. What happened to the Jewish man's clothes? They are gone – taken – and he was beaten up.

At the end of the day, when you take away all the status symbols - the type of watch, shoes, what kind of car (like a Tesla vs. a Messla) - it doesn't matter how big their house is, or if they live an apartment or a mobile home. It doesn't matter if their clothes are from Wal-mart or Nordstrom's.

Look beyond the differences and love from the heart. Racism is wrong. For any race to consider itself superior to another is evil and is the opposite of the compassion Jesus calls us to have. Any form of racism should not be tolerated in your heart or home or community or nation.

I think I was cured of this pretty early in my life because I actually experienced reverse racism. I grew up in four different states, but my high school years were spent in Mississippi.

The school I went to was 85% African-American. I was the only white guy on the basketball team. There were away games where the only white people in the building were me, the coach and my dad. My friends on the bench would glance at this sea of people in the bleachers and say "Micah, your dad is here." I was made fun of for being white; I can't repeat the names I was called at school. But I also had great friends and learned early on that at end of the day, we are all people; we all bleed red and are all loved by God unconditionally.

That is why we say here at Real Life, "Welcome Home." You are welcome at Real Life – no matter who you are, what you have done, how far away from God you feel, no matter where you live, what you drive, or the color of your skin. Welcome home.

We can get excited – and at times, *need* to get excited – marching for different causes. However, if we are not careful, we can go speak out against racism in a march or on social media and then we are not even nice to people in our own home. If we are not speaking with kindness and compassion to the people we are closest to, we have missed the point.

How many times do you let someone in your family

get on your nerves because of their differences? Come back to love – come back to compassion and choose kind words.

Choose to speak nice. Let's look at marriage. In the beginning of a relationship, there is so much love. They say to each other over and over again: "I love you so much!" And you'll hear about how opposites attract; God has a sense of humor; they don't even have the same favorite color. He likes to fish, she doesn't even like to eat fish. It doesn't matter, they love each other, right? What is happening? Initially, differences attract. But what tends to happen a few years later? "I love watching you sleep" turns into "You snore – go sleep on the couch." They start to get on our nerves. Let's choose a different path. Let's come back to compassion and look past the differences.

> *The Lord doesn't see things the way you see them. People judge by outward appearance, but the Lord looks at the heart.* (1 Samuel 16:7)

If that is where the Lord looks, then that is where you and I should look, too. And when you start looking at people's hearts – not their actions, not their outfits, not their differences – but when you see their heart, you'll have compassion because you realize everyone is wounded.

You stop seeing differences and you start seeing that the other person is hurting and wounded. This Samaritan comes by this man and he isn't selfish, he isn't too busy, he has empathy. He doesn't just see the need – he does something about it. Nice always speaks up and takes action. Notice this next verse:

> *Going over to him, the Samaritan soothed*
> *his wounds with olive oil and wine and*
> *bandaged them. Then he put the man on*
> *his own donkey and took him to an inn,*
> *where he took care of him.* (Luke 10:34)

When you stop highlighting differences and just start having compassion from your heart, you start to:

2. Heal wounds by meeting practical needs.

Practical needs go beyond what you would do for a pet. I am talking about more than food, water and shelter.

For instance, here are some practical needs every person in your life has:

Everyone needs attention – someone who will listen without judging, interrupting or trying to fix it. Someone who listens with their eyes and is not distracted, but focused.

Everyone needs affirmation – some type of acknowledgment that you did something well, encouragement, a word that lifts our spirits.

Everyone needs a friend – Someone who says, "I am here and not going anywhere." Someone who doesn't just promise but proves: "I will be by your side no matter what you do and no matter what happens."

By the way, God offers all of these; you have his undivided attention all day. He bends down to listen to your prayers, He goes before you and behind you, and He is with you. He will never leave you or forsake you.

God is the best source of your affirmation: the Bible is filled with encouragement. Jesus tells us to be strong and courageous and to not be afraid.

God is a friend that sticks closer than any other friend. Think about it, who really does love you and who will never reject you, leave you or forsake you? God has proven His love by the cross and promised His presence no matter what we face or go through.

When I choose to be nice, I am joining God in his ministry to you.

The Good Samaritan knows God cares for all people.

So, when he sees this wounded man in trouble, he seeks to help him. It is as if he is on a mission from God himself. Nice people realize they are the hands and feet of Jesus showing God's love and sharing God's love with a world in need.

When you realize everyone around you is wounded, you have to decide to go all in to help them. You don't just say you love people; you make the commitment. "I am going to be nice." Nice goes the extra mile – nice speaks the right words of comfort and hope, nice goes above and beyond.

I love the next verse in Luke:

> **The next day he handed the innkeeper two silver coins, telling him, 'Take care of this man. If his bill runs higher than this, I'll pay you the next time I'm here.'** (Luke 10:35)

He uses his words (and some coins) to encourage the innkeeper to take care of the man. The Good Samaritan has made the decision that we need to make ...

3. Be generous with your time, money and words.

Generosity flows from gratitude. Make speaking gratitude a daily habit. Choose to say to someone, "I am thankful you are in my life" or even "I am thankful for this opportunity to help you."

Begin by being grateful with your words to God. This is why we should be generous to God in prayer. Make it a daily habit to pray, "God, I am grateful for everything you have given me. I am giving back to you." Nice isn't just generous in the offering basket at church on Sunday; it is generous with the laundry basket, too:

"It's not my turn to wash the clothes." Or, "I'm not folding them; it's your turn to fold."

Hit pause to selfishness and busy-ness and a lack compassion! Lean in. Think about how you can be generous with your attention, your affirmation, your friendship.

How can you offer your attention at this moment? Put down your phone, turn off the TV – or at least pause it, push away from the computer screen.

There is this Family Circus cartoon where the kid is trying to get his dad's attention, and the dad is reading a book and watching TV. The kid says, "Dad, you aren't listening?!" and the dad says, "Yes I am." The kid replies, "Dad, I need you to listen with your *eyes*."

Listen with your eyes this week – people need attention.

Affirm – ask how your words can heal.

Be a friend – be there for someone else.

Everyone you meet is wounded. Just being nice and being compassionate can change your relationships. Then you don't take their words, actions and attitudes personally (your spouse is probably not angry at you – they are hurting, scared, and discouraged).

Heal wounds, don't cause them.

WHO IS YOUR NEIGHBOR? Go ahead and write it here; put their names in this book:

_____

Start with your spouse if you are married. Wife, husband, kids, friends, coworkers.

Want to change your relationship with these people you wrote down?

Start here. Choose nice.

BE NICE WITH THEM / SPEAK NICE TO THEM / DO NICE THINGS FOR THEM

> *"When I was a boy I used to think that strong meant having big muscles, great physical power; but the longer I live, the more I realize that real strength has much more to do with what is not seen. Real strength has to do with helping others."* – Fred Rogers

"Now which of these three would you say was a neighbor to the man who was attacked by bandits?" Jesus asked. The man replied, "The one who showed him mercy." Then Jesus said, "Yes, now go and do the same." (Luke 10:36-37)

PRAYER:

Father in Heaven, thank you for the mercy you have shown me. Help me to share mercy with others. Give me the patience to slow down and see the needs of the people in my life. Give me the strength to be nice, helping others with my words and actions. Remind me with each conversation that everyone I talk to is wounded. Today, give me your compassion for the people around me to heal wounds and not cause them. May my words be a blessing and soothe the hurt hearts I will encounter today.

JUST BE NICE

"

I close my letter with these last words: Be joyful. Grow to maturity. Encourage each other. Live in harmony and peace. Then the God of love and peace will be with you.

"

(2 Corinthians 13:11)

8

FIGHT FOR PEACE

Paul finishes his letter to the church in Corinth
with this personal plea: *Be joyful. Grow to
maturity. Encourage each other. Live in harmony
and peace. Then the God of love and peace will be with
you.* (*2 Corinthians 13:11*) I would like to close this book
with the same challenge: if you want to have harmony
in your relationships, choose to encourage people, love
everyone and be a peacemaker. This is going to require
work on your part. **You must be intentional with your
words and actions to live in peace.**

Let me offer one more example from Fred Rogers' life.
Remember in the previous chapter, we discovered
Mr. Rogers was an ordained Presbyterian minister?
He was a man who was intentional about sharing the
message of Jesus' love in real life situations to connect
people back to what really matters.

In the last chapter, I talked about what it means to be a good neighbor and the power of choosing to be nice. Now, we are going to see that Mr. Rogers was more than just a nice guy who spoke with kind words. He was intentional with everything he said and did to work for harmony so people could experience peace.

For instance, during one episode in 1969, Mr. Rogers talked about how hot it was outside. He filled a small plastic pool with water and put his feet in it. Then Mr. Clemens, the police officer of Mr. Rogers' neighborhood, comes by and Mr. Rogers asks him if he would like to soak his feet in the pool with him. Mr. Clemens was black. This is more than nice – this is the next level of nice. Mr. Rogers was a peacemaker. You see, back then, in 1969, Jim Crow policies were in affect; black and white segregation was everywhere. Swimming pools, for instance, had designated times for blacks and for whites. When people tried to protest this, there was violence all across the South.

Mr. Rogers was making a statement – the camera actually went to their feet and lingered on the shot for awhile – a pair of white feet and a pair of black feet in the same pool at the same time. No violence. No conflict. Just peaceful.

More than two decades later, in 1993, Mr. Rogers did a follow-up episode and recreated the same scene. He and Mr. Clemens actually shared a big laugh. Then something special happened: Mr. Rogers offered to help Clemens dry his feet off. Clemens would later recall that he felt so unworthy and it was the most loving, kind thing anyone had ever done for him.

It is amazing what happens when we choose nice. Pursuing peace is nice on another level; remember Mr. Rogers was an ordained Presbyterian minister. He was giving us an example based on the example of Jesus.

In Matthew 5, Jesus begins preaching what is known as the Sermon on the Mount – this sermon goes all the way through Matthew 7. Let's look at one statement Jesus makes in the introduction:

> **God blesses those who work for peace, for they will be called the children of God.** (Matthew 5:9)

These words of Jesus in themselves are simple and may seem easy to do. However, we have to be very careful and intentional to make sure our words are bringing people together and promoting harmony. Peace doesn't just happen; you and I have to work for peace. We live in a polarizing society – politics, school boards, HOAs, sports, fantasy football draft parties – all can be very polarizing. It is almost like society is teaching us to choose a side and then attempt to be as negative as we can about the people on the opposite side.

Jesus says to work for peace, promote love with your words, look for common ground, get your feet in the same pool, wash each others feet.

We need to be peacemakers in our society. Let's start with the relationships closest to us, because that is where the most conflict potentially happens.

Have you ever gotten into a fight on the way to church? It happens. The conflict starts with something small, but then begins to build. By the time we pull into the church parking lot the fight is a back and forth tennis match going front seat to back seat and then back to front seat. No one knows what they are arguing about but everyone is involved and then you get out of the car. You immediately smile and greet a complete stranger with a peaceful voice, "Good morning! How are you?" as if nothing was wrong. That happens in church parking lots across the country. Conflict is inevitable. Peace must be pursued.

Jesus didn't say, "Blessed are those who love peace." Everybody loves peace. Or, "Blessed are the peaceable"

– those who never get disturbed by anything. Working for peace is a courageous action. It's not avoiding. It's not running from the problem. It's not pretending it doesn't exist. It's not saying, "I don't want to talk about it." None of us like conflict, so we avoid it, postpone it, put it off, but it only gets bigger.

Jesus didn't say, "Blessed are those who are passive in order to keep the peace." When you always give in and let the other person have their own way, you let people run over you. That's passivity. Jesus was a very controversial person; he stood his ground on a number of issues that mattered to him. Jesus is not saying be a doormat and always give in so that there will never be conflict.

Jesus says blessed are those who work for peace, who make peace happen - who actively seek to resolve conflict, meet the issues head on, and don't ignore it.

Jesus is not calling us to cause conflict – he is calling us to cause peace. He is pleased with peacemakers not troublemakers. Speaking of troublemakers - is this you? Do you say to yourself, "I like to fight, I am good at it, I am mad and not talking to seven people right now and that will teach them!"

Unresolved conflict blocks your fellowship with God.

The Bible says you cannot have close fellowship with God and be out of fellowship with other people at the same time.

If I tell you I have a grudge against you, and resentment toward you, and bitterness because of something you did, and I am mad because of something you said, and pretty much to sum it up, I hate you – but I love God – I love to sing worship music. (What? Does that make any sense?)

> **If someone says, "I love God," but hates a fellow believer, that person is a liar; for if we don't love people we can see, how can we love God, whom we cannot see?** (1 John 4:20)

Think about communion. The same root word for communion is where we get our word community. It's supposed to bring everyone together as one body. The bread and the cup aren't just about you and God – they are about the people around you, all of us. The best decision you can make today is to draw close to God. That is why Jesus came – so we could draw close to God. But the more we love God, the more we should love each other.

The cross has a vertical beam and a horizontal beam. Jesus died to bring peace between you and your Heavenly Father (vertical), but also to bring peace between you and the people around you (horizontal). If you're growing close to God and the other person is growing close to God, its inevitably going to pull the two of you closer together. On the other hand, when you're out of fellowship with people (horizontal to you), then that is an indication that you could be out of fellowship with God (vertically).

Let's get even more practical. Why should I choose to speak harmony and peace? **Anger and bitterness prevent my happiness.**

Everybody wants to be happy; anger and bitterness short-circuit that pursuit. Resentment is just dumb. When you get resentful, it monopolizes your attention. That's all you can think about, right? That other person who wronged you? They're having a great time and you're the one who's upset. You have to let go and forgive them and forgive yourself.

Do you realize that unresolved conflict actually blocks your fellowship with God? It prevents answered prayer; it hinders your happiness. If you're still bitter, if you're still frustrated over it, it is still unresolved. The Bible says:

> *You are only hurting yourself with your anger.*
> *(Job 18:4 GN)*

Do you want to be happy? Then forgive. Let go of bitterness. I love how the Basic English Version translates Jesus' words:

> **Happy are the peacemakers: for they will be named sons of God.** (*Matthew 5:9 BBE*)

What is that first word? Happy! Happiness is the result of working toward peace. You can have peace knowing that you said all you could say and did all you could do to bring harmony to the relationship.

If you want peace in your relationships, you have to work for it.

How do you work for PEACE?

We are called to be peacemakers. The path to peace will ultimately bring us happiness. But how do we do it? Below I offer five principles that are an acrostic for the word P-E-A-C-E. This will make these principles easier to remember, but it is still hard to do.

The first thing we need to do is:

Pursue peace now.

Jesus encourages us to take the initiative. If someone does something that hurt you, or if you did something to hurt them, *you* take the initiative. Either way! Don't wait for them to make the first move. Watch this. It doesn't matter if I'm the offended or the offender, it's always my move:

> *If you are about to offer your gift to God at the altar and there you remember that your brother has something against you, leave your gift there in front of the altar. (You are not off the hook to give – come back and give.)*
> *(Matthew 5:23-24 GN)*

Go at once and make peace with your brother, and then come back and offer your gift to God. In other words, **we must automatically and actively speak words of peace.**

Always take the initiative. Why? Because Jesus said so. You take the initiative. Because you're more mature. Go first. Pursue peace now. Conflict is not resolved accidentally. It doesn't resolve itself. You must intentionally deal with it. When do you deal with it? "... at once ..." Do it now. Don't postpone it. If you avoid or delay, it only grows worse. The longer I wait to resolve a conflict, the more difficult it's going to be to resolve it. Take Matthew 5 and Mark 11. One of them says that when somebody offends you, go to them; the other says when you offend them, you go to them. Either way, you take the initiative. If you want to be peacemaker, pursue peace NOW.

Empathize with their feelings.
When you sit down to talk, the tendency is to make the conversation about you. If you are not careful, you focus on how *you* are feeling and how *they* hurt you and what *you* think the problem is. Instead, ask how *they* are feeling, and try to feel what *they* feel. This takes some work, because you will have to be unselfish and humble.

> *Don't be selfish ... be humble ... Don't look out only for your own interests, but take an interest in others, too.* (Philippians 2:3-4)

Notice these three words from Paul's letter: "take an interest." These three words shift the focus from you to the other person. The word in Greek is the word "scopos" from which we get the word scope. It means to pay attention to their needs. When I am upset, who am I thinking about? Me. I am focused on *my* needs, *my* hurts, and how you hurt *me*. I don't care about you. God says to reverse that. Hold a peace conference and think about what their needs are, what can I do to help them? Focus on *their* needs, not your own needs.

Parents have to be peacemakers a lot, working through all types of conflict from tug-of-war over toys to in-house fighting. They need to listen to their kids, be sensitive and empathize with their needs. Why are these kids arguing over this? One of the values of conflict is when you solve it, it usually leads to greater intimacy because you understand them better. You've been listening.

This leads us to the third principle of being a peacemaker:

Attack the problem, not the person.

You can't focus on fixing the problem and fixing the blame at the same time. It's impossible. If you go to the meeting thinking you're going to blame the other person, then forget it. If you are going into the conversation to win, you will lose the relationship. A wise person – a mature person – attacks the problem, not the person.

> *The wisdom from above is first of all pure.*
> *It is also peace loving, gentle at all times, and*
> *willing to yield to others. It is full of mercy and*
> *the fruit of good deeds. It shows no favoritism*
> *and is always sincere. (James 3:17 NLT)*

What happens at an intersection when no one yields? A lot of accidents, a lot of damage. We have to be willing to yield with our words. Tone it down; tone down your voice, your mannerisms. Tone down the sarcasm, the cynicism. Remove the walls you are building. Engage your mind before you engage your mouth. Be sincere, not sarcastic. Don't criticize, condemn or compare. Attack the problem, not the person.

As hard as we try to bring peace, and as much as we desire harmony in our relationships, sometimes it doesn't work. The reason is it takes two people to resolve a conflict. Both parties must be humble and willing to move toward restoration. However, we still must embrace this fourth principle:

Cooperate as much as possible.

Be a bridge-builder and not a bridge destroyer. Go with the spirit of compromise: What can we agree on? What can we do together? The hallmark of a Christian ought to be your ability to get along with other people. It's not how much you pray, read the Bible, sing, or give (those are all great things to do). But here is the big question: do you get along with other people?

> ***Do all that you can to live in peace***
> ***with everyone.*** *(Romans 12:18)*

Focus on the phrase, "all that you can".

There are some people you can't get along with. No matter where you go on this earth, there are people who refuse to be nice and are bent on arguments, dissension and conflict. They are just not going to get along. They are irregular people. Remember, Jesus had enemies. Even the Son of God couldn't make everyone happy.

Do everything possible to work toward peace. Warning: peace always has a price. If you want peace in your home, in your marriage, in your relationships, there is always going to be a price. It costs your self-ego. It costs your self-centeredness and your selfishness. You've got to be willing to give in. You have to be willing to say these humbling words: 'Maybe my wife is right.' 'Maybe my husband does have a point.' 'Maybe my kid has a legitimate gripe.' 'Maybe my parents do know what they're talking about.'

If you want to be a peacemaker, you've got to give up your pride and your ego, and choose humility. That is what it costs to achieve peace. You have to be willing to say the three most difficult words in the English language: "I was wrong." The two most difficult words in the English language: "I'm sorry". The five most difficult? "I'm sorry. I was wrong." Seven? "I'm sorry. I was wrong, a lot." That's compromise.

Eric Seagle's book *Love Story* was made into a movie. The book claims, "Love means never having to say you're sorry." That is dead wrong! Love means saying you're sorry! Over and over. In relationships, you get hurt and you hurt other people. Accidentally or intentionally, you wound them with your words or actions. Saying, "I'm sorry" with sincerity and consistency will help you plant seeds of peace.

Peacemakers will plant seeds of peace and reap a harvest of righteousness. (James 3:18 NLT)

The current condition of your relationships is directly tied to the seeds you have planted in recent months or even years. If you don't like the crop around your feet, then change the seed that is in your bag. Start to sow different seeds. Sow words that promote harmony. Be patient. Give the relationship time to heal. Healthy relationships are grown over time with intentional deposits of peaceful words.

You reap what you sow. Choose to sow peace. If you want people to cooperate with you, you have to cooperate. If you want people to be nice to you, you've got to be nice to them. If you want people to compromise with you, you've got to compromise with them. Whatever you're dishing out is what you're getting back. If you've got conflict in your family, somehow you're dishing some of it out. It takes two to have a fight. So you look and say, "What can I do? What seeds am I planting?" If you are always planting seeds of griping, complaining, arguing, hassling, and putting down your friend or family member, guess what you're going to reap? Conflict.

Whatever seeds you're planting in your relationships is what you're going to grow. Start planting seeds of peace and compromise. Empathize with their feelings and take the initiative, don't wait for them. Go to them. Do everything you can to bring harmony to the relationship, which leads us to the last principle:

Emphasize reconciliation, not resolution.
Reconciliation means to reestablish a relationship. It does not mean you resolve all the problems. A lot of times, there are some legitimate, honest differences between husbands and wives, employees and bosses, men and women. There are major differences between men and women. We just think differently.

Reconciliation means you bury the hatchet, not the issue. You keep talking about it, but you talk about it in harmony. You can disagree, agreeably. **You can walk arm-in-arm together without necessarily seeing eye-to-eye.** You can have reconciliation without having resolution of every problem. Reconciliation focuses on the relationship. Resolution focuses on the issue.

First and foremost, focus on reconciliation of the relationship and often, the issue will resolve itself, because now two people are working in the same direction to resolve it. Bring your hearts together first, then you can work on putting your heads together.

> **God has reconciled us to Himself through Christ and has given us the ministry of reconciliation.**
> *(2 Corinthians 5:18 NIV)*

Reconciliation is a prerequisite for worship. When you come to church and you're ready to give your offering and you remember somebody has something against you, it says, "Go, get that right and then come back." Nothing can substitute for reconciliation. Not giving, not sharing, not reading the Bible. If you're having a hard time getting an answer to prayer, maybe you'd better check out your relationships.

How do you know that it's not settled? Do you still remember it? Are you still thinking about it? Are you still rehearsing it in your mind over and over and it still hurts today? Then it's not resolved.

The synonym for peacemaker is reconciler - one who brings people together. God sent Jesus Christ to bring us to Him so we could have peace with God. God is the original peacemaker.

Jesus is the Prince of Peace. What He has modeled, He now wants us to do with other people. When you help restore relationships, you're doing what God would do. When you help bring people together who have been estranged, that's the most Christ-like thing you could do. The ministry of reconciliation. When God looks down on you and you're taking the initiative to restore harmony in that marriage or harmony in that office or with that parent or child or estranged relative – when you're doing that, God looks down on you and says, "That's my girl!" or "That's my boy!" That person is a child of God.

God is pleased with peacemakers; it is as if He is saying, "They are doing exactly what I would do if I were in that situation." Who can be a peacemaker? You can. Anybody can become a peacemaker. But first you must have peace on the inside of you. You can't spread peace if you're at war on the inside. Only what you have can you offer to others. When you discover peace with God, then you can become a peacemaker.

> *And let the peace that comes from Christ*
> *rule in your hearts. For as members of one body*
> *you are called to live in peace.* (*Colossians 3:15*)

Note the word "rule" in that passage. The word in

Greek is the same word from which we get the word "umpire". That means somebody who calls the shots, who keeps you in boundaries, a referee, somebody who keeps the game going and keeps it in focus. He's saying, "Let the peace of God umpire your heart." When you have peace with God, then you get the peace of God. When you have the peace of God then you can have peace with other people. That's the order. It all begins with this decision: let the peace of God rule in your heart.

Peace comes when you find the most important relationship you can ever have in life. Your Creator designed you to meet Him, to know Him and to have a relationship with Him. I'm not talking about religion, I'm talking about relationship. A relationship with God is the only source of genuine peace in this life. Then, when you have that peace in your heart, you can speak peace, pursue peace and be at peace with others.

If you have not begun a relationship with God, I'd encourage you to do it today. Open your life to Christ and invite His peace in and experience the Prince of Peace. Many of you have made that decision at some point in your life or even while reading this book. So my question to all of us is:

What do you want to be remembered for? What do you want people to write on your tombstone? Peacemaker? or Troublemaker? What do you have a reputation for? Peacemaker? or Troublemaker?

It's never too late to become a Peacemaker. Start today.

St. Francis of Assisi used to pray ***"Lord, make me an instrument of Thy peace."*** That's a great prayer to pray. Wherever there are hostilities, let me bring peace. Let me do the thing that is the most Christ-like thing I could do – bring people together. Bring harmony where there is disharmony, restitution where there is conflict. Every time you go out and win somebody to Christ, every time you tell somebody about the story of the cross, you're being a peacemaker. Every time you tell a friend or somebody at work, "Jesus loves you," and you introduce them to God's love, you are being a peacemaker.

Peacemakers choose words that are positive, words that are Gospel (which simply means Good News), words that heal, and words that life up. Perhaps the most important word for peacemakers to remember is *forgiveness.*

Do you have the peace of Christ ruling in your heart? Have you been looking for the missing peace?

For Christ himself is our way of peace.
He has made peace between us Jews and
you Gentiles by making us all one family,
breaking down the wall of contempt that used
to separate us. By His death He ended the
angry resentment between us ... and at last
there was peace. As parts of the same body,
our anger against each other has disappeared,
for both of us have been reconciled to God.
And so the feud ended at last at the cross.
(*Ephesians 2:12-14 LB*)

Instead of throwing words that injure like sticks and stones, sow seeds of healing and hope with everything that comes out of your mouth. Be a peacemaker. Instead of building walls made of anger, build bridges made of love. This is hard to do. It takes work and intentional effort. At the end of the day, only the Prince of Peace can give you the power and the strength to bring peace to your relationships.

Before you try to change the condition of your relationships, humble yourself before God and ask Him to change you.

Before you speak peaceful words, you need to surrender your heart to the Prince of Peace.

I encourage you to pray this daily prayer St. Francis of Assisi spoke each morning. The words of this prayer, said with a sincere heart, will change your heart and your words.

PRAYER:

Lord, make me an instrument of your peace. Where there is hatred, let me sow love; where there is injury, pardon; where there is discord, union; where there is doubt, faith; where there is despair, hope; where there is darkness, light; and where there is sadness, joy.

O Divine Master, grant that I may not so much seek to be consoled, as to console; to be understood, as to understand; to be loved, as to love. For it is in giving that we receive, it is in pardoning that we are pardoned, and it is in dying that we are born to eternal life. Amen.

"

*You can change the course
of your life and someone else's
life with your words.*"

(Anonymous)

CONCLUSION: BULLETS OR SEEDS

We discovered a lot about words in this book. We learned that words are the most powerful force available to humanity. We also realized that we can choose to use this force constructively with words of encouragement, or destructively using words of despair. Words have energy and power with the ability to help, to heal, to hinder, to hurt, to harm, to humiliate and to humble.

You can change the course of your life and someone else's life with your words.

Considering the powerful force of what we say, we have come face-to-face with the responsibility of needing to discipline ourselves to speak in a way that conveys respect, gentleness and humility. One of the clearest signs of a mature person is their ability to use uplifting words that are helpful to all listeners. As Christians, we are called to be kind to all and speak words that are offer inspiration, enthusiasm and encouragement. We should never waste our words on trivial matters like coarse joking or gossiping about others; instead, we should choose helpful, healing words that light up this dark world.

In this book, we also learned certain principles that should guide all of our communication with others. Always speak the truth, avoid prideful boasting, be kind in how you say it, don't yell or scream, never let feelings drive your words, don't use your words to manipulate others, and most importantly do not use words to insult or belittle anyone.

In his book, Love as a Way of Life, Gary Chapman uses the vivid metaphor for words as being either 'bullets or seeds'. If we use our words as bullets with a feeling of superiority and condemnation, we are not going to be able to restore a relationship to love. However, if we use our words as seeds with a feeling of supportiveness and sincere good will, we can rebuild a relationship in positive and life-affirming ways. This means – even when we need to have a difficult conversation about something – we must focus on the solution, being willing to listen patiently, speak gently, tell the truth in love, and be willing to empathize with someone else's point of view. How we interact with someone – including what we say – allows seeds of love and peace to be planted in every interaction.

Words are bullets or seeds, they have the power to build people up, confine people to where they are, or break people down. Choose your words carefully before you let them leave your voicebox. As Joyce Meyer points out, "Words are containers for power, you choose what kind of power they carry." Words can wound someone or help them grow. Words are poison or fruit – you choose.

As Christians it is our job to encourage and bless people with our words. The quickest way to change your words and the best way to shift how you talk is to talk to God as you begin each day. Using your words in prayer is the first step to changing how you use your words in every day relationships. Read the Bible every morning and allow His Word to be a seed in your heart so you can see your words as seeds planted in others. This is why this book ends with a 21-day prayer devotional. Praying to God and focusing on Him each day will change your life and your words.

Real Life began with 30 key leaders and their families praying and fasting for three months asking for God's direction, wisdom and power. We believed from those early days what Ephesians 3:20 says, "Now all glory to God, who is able, through His mighty power at work within us, to accomplish infinitely more than we might ask or think." These words inspire me every time I read them.

Since the beginning of Real Life we have always prayed, "God do what only YOU can do so only YOU get the credit for it." Prayer is how our church began and it is how you should begin not just every year, but every situation. I believe as you walk through this devotional each day you will apply the small changes in your words that will create big changes in your relationships.

Why should you do this 21-day devotional? First, It will help your relationship with God, and your relationship with God is the most important relationship in your life. Second, it will help you in your relationship with others. Any relationship you value will take work and attention in order to stay healthy and grow. Third, you can only change *you*. You can't force anyone else to change. In order to change the world or a relationship, start with your heart. This devotional will help you become the best you can be and give you the faith to bring out the best in others.

A 21-DAY DEVOTIONAL
Based on Sticks and Stones

DAY 1: YOUR CHOICE

Today begins a new year and has the potential to be
a brand new you with one simple, powerful choice.
Changing the words that come our of your mouth.
Our words are OUR choice. To kill or give life with
words is 100% our coice. 'I'm going to kill their dream
right now'; 'I'm going to kill their self-esteem right now.'
Or 'I'm going to bring life to this situation.' 'I'm going to
bring fruit to this.'

You actually get to choose the words that come out of
your mouth. You have 100% responsibility for them,
right? They're not forced on you. They are your choice,
to bring life and value to the people and the relationships
around you That's what you were designed to do. And
they were designed to run on our life-giving words.

Let's evaluate our words. Are they positive, or negative?
Today, begin a fast ... from negative words. For the next
21 days, only say positive words. Your life will change
and your relationships will change. God designed us
to say positive words and run on the positive words of
others. I don't care how great the relationship looks on
the outside – if you aren't putting the right words into a
relationship; if we are not communicating the way God

intended for us to; it's going to go downhill. Quickly.

Relationships can elevate quickly as well – want to change a relationship? Choose positive words. Want to change your life? Change your words. What comes out of your mouth is 100% your choice.

PRAYER:
Heavenly Father, right now I decide to fast from all negative words. For the next 21 days, help me to only say what is positive, encouraging and uplifting. Your Scriptures tell me that "out of the overflow of the heart the mouth speaks." So, change my heart so my words will change. Thank you for the life and the grace you give to start this new year with a new commitment and a new chance to change. I choose to say only life-giving words to everyone I interact with today. In Jesus name, Amen.

DAY 2: EVERY WORD COUNTS

And I tell you this, you must give an account on judgment day for every idle word you speak. *(Matthew 12:36)*

Jesus got everybody's attention with this statement. Every teenager texting to friends; every child talking to their parent; every parent who has lectured their children – every word.

Jesus says that God will review every word at the end of your life when you meet him face to face. Why? Because words are a big deal – they are powerful.

Did you know that words can hurt? And it can happen suddenly. You weren't expecting it but all of a sudden somebody says something and it stings. All of a sudden you open up your email and somebody's got a special gift for you. Just kind of threw up words all over you, and what they said is very painful. Or you opened up Facebook and someone left a nice post. It's cryptic, but you know it's about you. Or someone tweets something negative about you. All of a sudden, your day changes.

Words cause pain. Words can also cause healing. Decide to bring healing and not hurt today.

PRAYER:
Heavenly Father, thank you for this reminder that one day I will answer to you for what I say. Forgive me for the hurtful things I have said to others and about others in the past. Also, you know the hurtful things people have said to me or about me. Heal me of that hurt. Hurt people, hurt people so heal my heart so I don't hurt others with my words. Help me to heal and not hurt with what I say today. When I see you face to face, I want to celebrate

with you the people that I was able to help and heal with my words. In Jesus name, Amen.

DAY 3: RECEIVE AND SPEAK GRACE

Indeed, we all make many mistakes. For if we could control our tongues, we would be perfect and could also control ourselves in every other way. *(James 3:2)*

You have – I have – every person reading this has – made mistakes with their words. The reason we need this book is because ALL of us have messed up one relationship or another with words. We have chosen to go negative and not positive with what we say. And when we go negative, we mess up our relationships and they all go negative, too.

Now here's the great news: Welcome to Real Life. We've all made mistakes. Welcome to Real Life. God can forgive. There's grace for you. And you're not reading this now to beat yourself up over what you wish you could take back. 'I wish I hadn't said that.' 'I wish I didn't post that.' 'I wish I hadn't emailed that.' But today, we can all hit 'reset' by grace, and allow Jesus and what he did on the cross to forgive us.

Let's say, "You know what? I'm going to start changing RIGHT NOW and I'm not going the way I've always gone with my words.

PRAYER:

Heavenly Father, I have made mistakes with my words. Thank you for your forgiveness and grace and that your Scriptures say, "your mercy and compassion is new every morning". Today, because of your grace, I hit "reset". Jesus, thank you that you were beaten up on that cross so I can stop beating myself up. Fill my heart with your love and grace. Give me the power to change. Help my words to be full of grace and love today because I have received your grace and love in my heart. In Jesus name, Amen.

DAY 4: WORDS SET YOUR DIRECTION

We can make a large horse go wherever we want by means of a small bit in its mouth. And a small rudder makes a huge ship turn wherever the pilot chooses to go, even though the winds are strong. *(James 3:3-4)*

Just like a small rudder on a boat.

In case you haven't seen a rudder lately – know that it is quite small compared to the whole boat. Usually you can't even see the rudder – but this tiny mechanism in the back of boat tells this big ship where to go. James is illustrating to us that in the same way you can say something very small to someone that changes the course of their life and moves them in God's direction. Your words turn direction of your life by what you say. If you say, 'I"ll never amount to anything' or 'I'll never get there' or 'this could never change,' you're literally turning your heart that way by what you just said. How about this instead? 'I'm not going to give up' and 'God's gonna come through' and 'There's always hope' and 'God can move mountains' and 'I'm moving toward a dream that God's given me.'

The words literally direct my heart.

PRAYER:
Heavenly Father, help me to be careful with my words. Help me to remember that my words set the direction of my life. What I talk about is what I am drawn to and what will come to pass. Since words direct my heart, help me to guard my words so I can guard my heart. Especially when I talk about what is going to happen in my life or those I love. Your Scriptures promise me that your plan is to prosper me and give me a future and a hope. So, help me to speak hope into every situation and blessing into every circumstance. Give me a fresh vision and hope to speak over my life, my family, my friends and my workplace. In Jesus name, Amen.

DAY 5: HOW YOU SAY IT

A gentle answer deflects anger,
but harsh words make tempers flare.
(*Proverbs 15:1*)

Some of you need to decide today that you are going to work on how you say things – how you come across. Parents give this speech all the time to kids who get in trouble, "It isn't what you said, it is how you said it."

We have to be careful how we say it.

One university study has shown that communication is only 7% words. Only 7% is words. Did you know that 55% of communication is your body language? 38% is the tone of your voice – <u>how</u> you say something.

This means we can say the right thing the wrong way.

Ask God to help you be gentle with not just your words, but with your tone and your body language.

PRAYER:
Heavenly Father, help me not to say the first thing that comes in my mind. Help me not to speak out of anger or frustration. Give me the strength to answer gently. Give me the humility to change my approach and my delivery. Help me to communicate love with what I say but

also with how I say it. Help me to diffuse conflicts and arguments by giving a gentle answer. Help kindness be the hallmark of how I interact with people today. In Jesus name, Amen.

DAY 6: NICE IS SPELLED L-O-V-E

The man answered, "'You must love the Lord your God with all your heart, all your soul, all your strength, and all your mind.' And, 'Love your neighbor as yourself.' "Right!" Jesus told him. "Do this and you will live!" *(Luke 10:27-29)*

Did you grew up watching *Mr. Rogers Neighborhood*? I asked that question at our staff retreat and there were people from their 50's down to their 20's who answered, "Yes". Whether you watched him or not, or liked him or not, this guy was on TV for more than 30 years, in one of the longest-running programs in television history with more than 870 episodes. That's almost five times as many as *Friends*! Why did so many people tune in? What was it about his show that kept kids and their parents coming back?

There a lot of four-letter words out there these days, but we need more of this one – NICE. What made him so nice? What was the secret?

His favorite number was 143. One episode he explained that "I" has one letter, "love" has four letters and "you" has three letters. 1.4.3. What caused him to be so NICE (a four letter word) was another four letter word: LOVE.

Did you know that this whole idea of being nice to your neighbors didn't come from Mr. Rogers? He was a pastor – he knew that the concept actually came from Jesus.

Today, here is your assignment. Choose five people in your family or close friends who are like family and say these three, powerful words: "I love you".

PRAYER:
Jesus, thank you for showing me what love is by dying on the cross for me. Today, I choose to love you. I give you all my heart, soul, mind and strength. Help me to love others the way you love them. Help me to see them the way you see them. Give me patience, kindness and compassion for the people in my life. Today, I choose to be nice by your grace and for your glory. In Jesus name, Amen.

DAY 7: HIT THE PAUSE BUTTON

Understand this, my dear brothers and sisters:
You must all be quick to listen, slow to speak,
and slow to get angry. (James 1:19)

Some verses don't need a lot of explanation. What is
James saying? Hurry up and listen. Keep your mouth
closed. Keep your emotions in check. Hit pause before
you run your mouth. For some of us, we need work on
hitting the pause button. Especially when you are
angry. When anger is stirring up, don't say the first
thing that comes to your mind! When you are really
angry, don't say the second thing that comes in your
mind. Back up, hit pause.

We don't exactly live in a nation of listeners, do we?
'Here what I'm saying!' And if you can't hear it, 'I'm
going to say it louder!' We struggle with listening.
It's sort of built into our culture. Back in the day,
Will Rogers said this about Congress: "Congress is so
strange. A man gets up to speak and says nothing.
Nobody listens. And then everybody disagrees."

That's what we're like. Listening is not our natural
preference. Most of us would rather be speaking than
listening. You could really do yourself a big favor with

words if you'll just pause and listen before you speak. Pause and step back and say, 'I'm going to listen."

PRAYER:

Heavenly Father, help me to be a better listener. Help me to not just open my ears but open my heart to what the other person is saying. Help me to listen with my eyes to see their point of view, their feelings and their perspective. Even if what they are saying is hard to hear, even if I don't agree with what they are saying, help me to hit pause. Please help me to stop getting so angry and help me when I do get angry to calm down BEFORE I speak. Give me the strength to be quick to listen, slow to speak and slow to become angry. In Jesus name, Amen.

DAY 8: PRAY BEFORE YOU SPEAK

May the words of my mouth and the meditation of my heart be pleasing to you, O Lord, my Rock and my Redeemer. *(Psalm 19:14)*

Who are you trying to please with your words? At the end of the day, the only thing that matters is – was God pleased with what I said and how I said it.

This Psalm contains a prayer that I hope you'll pray every day. I pray this prayer every time before I get on stage to speak on Sunday mornings. I pray this prayer every morning during the week. Even with this prayer, I know I blow it. I know I do. And I have. But I pray this prayer because I take very seriously what I Say and I need God's help so I have a shot at saying the right words. I want to ask you to pray the prayer yourself every day.

I would just ask you to try it. Pray this prayer before you get out of bed. I ask you to pray this prayer before you interact with anyone in
your house ... When you're in the parking lot about to walk into your school or to your job. ... And before you get on Facebook or Twitter. Start right now, try it today and see how it helps you. We all need God's help to please Him with our words.

PRAYER:
May the words of my mouth and the meditation of my heart be pleasing to you, O Lord, my Rock and my Redeemer. In Jesus name, Amen.

DAY 9: PART OF A COMPLETE BREAKFAST

A cheerful look brings joy to the heart; good news makes for good health. (*Proverbs 15:30 NLT*)

Nutrition Focused?
This is really amazing information. This is like a brand

new part of a complete breakfast commercial, right? What makes a complete breakfast? Cereal, four slices of toast, a gallon of orange juice, three eggs and a protein bar? What if the best thing for your kid's health is to start talking nice to them; to share positive to talk? I have a great new revoluntionary health program:

SPEAK GOOD NEWS.

As parents, we can get so focused on nutrition that we forget the biggest part of our kids complete breakfast; we forget their greatest need isn't a good breakfast, it is a good word from us.

PRAYER:

Heavenly Father, help me to bring health to those around me by what I say. Help me to focus on good news. Help me to tune out bad news. Help me to share good news. Help me to remember that good news makes for good health. May I share Bible verses with other people and talk about Jesus and his love more. Help me speak words cheer and joy to the hearts of people who hear me. Help me to talk about you more – how good you are, how you are blessing me, how you give me every good thing I have, how you guide me. Today, let my words be life-giving. In Jesus name, Amen.

DAY 10: PSSSST. HAVE YOU HEARD GOSSIP IS DANGEROUS?

*Their lives became full of every kind of wickedness,
sin, greed, hate, envy, murder, quarreling, deception,
malicious behavior, and gossip.*

(*Romans 1:29*)

Do you notice that gossip is on the same list as murder?
I don't have a gun in my bag; I don't have a grenade. I'm
not going to kill anybody. But words can kill people
by killing their reputation; killing their dreams; killing
their character; destroying things around them; mess
up all kinds of things. And we think that it's not a big
deal. But it causes guilt, just like you took somebody
out and buried him in the backyard. It can be overwhelming to look back and say, 'I can't believe I did
that.' And we try to make it look nice. We put glitter on
it when we put a little polka dots on gossip and call it a
prayer request, etc. It is still gossip.

So how about we focus on the Gospel, not on Gossip?
Every person needs GOSPEL. Nobody needs gossip.
Everyday, we make the choice. Gospel? or Gossip?

The word GOSPEL simply means GOOD NEWS.
GOSPEL = GOOD NEWS ABOUT GOD

Gospel – literally means good news.

GOSSIP = BAD NEWS ABOUT PEOPLE

PRAYER:

Heavenly Father, forgive me for talking about people behind their back. I realize words can kill. Forgive me for repeating negative news about others. From now on, keep me from gossip. Keep me from sharing it and keep me from hearing it. Help me not to talk about people. Give me opportunities today to brag on you and tell people the good news about you. Help me to AVOID gossip; help me to ADVANCE the Gospel. In Jesus name, Amen.

DAY 11: FORGIVENESS

Do not repay anyone evil-for-evil. Be careful to do what is right in the eyes of everybody. If it is possible, as far as it depends on you, live at peace with everyone. Do not take revenge, my friends, but leave room for God's wrath, for it is written: "It is mine to avenge; I will repay," says the Lord. (Romans 12:17-19)

"I forgive you." These may be the hardest three words to say, but are also the most powerful. God can use these words to set you free and heal your soul. God knows the people who have hurt you. He saw it and He cares. The Bible says one day he will settle the score. There is a heaven and there is a hell, there is a judgement day. He has far more resources to settle the score than you do. He says you cannot recover from your hurt as long as you are seeking revenge.

Revenge is big business. Take for example Netflix. I searched for movies with themes about revenge. Can you guess how many there were? 336! Think about these:

Gunslingers // Jaws // Star Wars
Transformers // Ninjas

Yes, revenge is big business, but revenge doesn't work. It always backfires. It keeps the hurt alive.

There is only one way you will ever get the relief you are looking for – that is forgiveness. Forgiveness is not saying it didn't hurt.

Forgiveness is not denying that evil is done in this world. Forgiveness is not becoming best friends again. Forgiveness is letting go so it doesn't hurt you anymore and letting God take care of the justice part.

PRAYER:
Heavenly Father, forgive me and help me to forgive others. As I reflect on how much you have forgiven me, as I look to the cross today, I am reminded of your mercy and grace

for me. How can I hold a grudge, when you showed me so much love. I choose to not seek revenge or repay evil for evil. I let go. I forgive. Heal me. Show me how to pursue peace in today. Help me to be a peacemaker with my words. In Jesus name, Amen.

DAY 12: GOD'S WORD & OUR WORDS HEAL

He sent out his word and healed them, snatching them from the door of death. *(Psalm 107:20)*

Speak Bible verses and gratitude over those you are closest to. Healing begins when we read God's Word, repeat God's Word, and express gratitude for God's gifts in our lives. My advice? Read God's Word and pray for others every day. Use prayer as healing words over every relationship in your life.

Married Couples: Pray out loud with your spouse. Try it one time this week. Hold hands when you're doing it and just say, "God, thank you for my spouse. Bless them. May your will be done in their heart. And God, thank you for the relationship we have, and help us to grow toward you."

Parents: Pray over your kids out loud before they go to sleep. Make sure the last thing your kids hear is not

'Did you do your homework? Okay, good-bye,' and close the door. No! Go by their bed. Kneel down and say, "God, thank you for this child. Bless them. I thank you that you love them, too. You have a plan - a purpose - that is beyond anything they can possibly imagine. You're going to do great things for them. They believe it. May you bless them for it."

Pray with your friends. Get together with your friends, and pray out loud with them. "God, thank you for our friendship. We just pray out loud to get the Gospel into their lives, and it will heal them."

PRAYER:
Heavenly Father, thank you. Thank you for a new day. Thank you for the gift of life. Help me to not focus on all of the problems and trouble this day may hold; help to focus on your Presence and Peace that walks through the day with me. Forgive me for taking things and especially people for granted. Every person in my life is a gift from you and special to me. Help me to be more grateful. Help me to say "thank you" to others more often. Help all my words be fueled by a grateful spirit and a thankful heart. In Jesus' name, Amen.

DAY 13: FAITH, HOPE & LOVE

When the true message, the Good News, first came to you, you heard about the hope it offers. So your faith and love are based on what you hope for, which is kept safe for you in heaven. (Colossians 1:5 GN)

You need one of these three words. Some of you have not placed your faith in God. You haven't received Jesus as your personal Lord and savior. You know about him, and you're 'religious', but do you have a relationship with him today? Place your faith in God who sent his son who died on a cross, who rose again, and who wants to live in your heart.

And what about love? We live in a world that sings about love; that has whole radio stations and music streams committed to love songs, but doesn't really know what love is. This is how we know what love is: Jesus Christ laid down his life for us, and they'll know that we are his disciples if we love each other. I'm going to encourage you to say 'I love you' a lot more often to the people that you actually love. If you're married, say 'I love you' before you leave for the day or before you get off the phone with them. Every time. Tell your kids you love them. Tell your parents you love them. Tell your friends you love them and share that love by just expressing it.

How about hope? Because we all live in a world that's very cynical and full of gossip, we need hope; we need people who love each other hold a confidence and share the Gospel. You may be facing a mountain right now; it seems really hard. God moves mountains and he can move that mountain in your life. There's always hope.

PRAYER:
Heavenly Father, I place my faith in you and what you can do today. Help me to share my faith in you with others who may be struggling. I place my life in the middle of your love today. Help me to share words of love to those who feel unlovable and neglected today. I place my hope in you today. Help me to share words of hope in this cynical world. Thank you that there is always hope for every situation I face. Thank you for the promise of heaven. May my words be filled with faith, hope and love today. In Jesus name, Amen.

DAY 14: GAME CHANGER

***Do everything without complaining
and arguing.*** *(Philippians 2:14)*

You think the SuperBowl is a big deal? This one verse

can change your life and the life of everyone around you! Parents, you're welcome. Warning: if you teach it to your kids, you actually have to do it, too. Every day, every hour, every minute, we choose one of two paths with our words.

Compliments: encouraging people, speaking words of life; – or – Complaints: which is like a poison.

The fact is, it is easy to slip into a mode of finding the negative things in life and complaining about them rather than finding the good things and complimenting those. Complaining is like a poison that really can ruin our lives and everything else. We can get negative. We can start to find things to complain about instead of looking for the good things that God is doing. It is easy to complain.

PRAYER:
Heavenly Father, this is such a short verse but it is so hard to do! When I focus on myself and what I want, I can start to argue. When I look at what others have and what I don't have, I can start to complain. Forgive me for being selfish and self-centered. I trust you to provide my needs. Today, I choose to focus on Jesus. I choose to focus on others. I choose to focus on Heaven. Help me to see the good in every situation and in every person. Give me words that

affirm instead of argue, words that compliment instead of complain. In Jesus name, Amen.

DAY 15: THE SECRET TO A MISERABLE LIFE

Jesus came to a certain village where a woman named Martha welcomed Him into her home. Her sister, Mary, sat at the Lord's feet, listening to what He taught. But Martha was distracted by the big dinner she was preparing. She came to Jesus and said, "Lord, doesn't it seem unfair to you that my sister just sits here while I do all the work? Tell her to come and help me." (Luke 10:38-40)

We welcome Jesus into our hearts and into our homes, and then we get distracted and complain about the people in our house. Jesus, my family is spending too much time with you, Jesus, this is ridiculous. From a negative heart overflows negative words, which generally become negative actions, which result in a miserable life.

Do you want to hate your job for the rest of your life? Then just complain. Complain about your commute, complain about the people that you work with that get on your nerves, complain about your boss who 'doesn't know anything', complain about the lousy benefit package, and how undervalued you are. If you complain about your job, you will hate your job. You want to hate your life? Complain about it.

PRAYER:

Heavenly Father, I invite you into my home today. Fill this place I live in with your Presence and Peace. Help me to be an example to my family and friends of someone who listens to the words of Jesus and speaks words that lift up. Forgive me for being too busy. Forgive me for complaining. Forgive me for neglecting my time with you. Right now, I invite you to not just fill my home, but fill my heart. As you fill me with life and love, may that life and love spill out on everyone I interact with today by what I say and share with them. In Jesus name, Amen.

DAY 16: ENCOURAGE 10 PEOPLE, TODAY!

Now get up! Go out there and thank them for what they did. If you don't ... you won't even have one man left on your side tomorrow morning. *(2 Samuel 19:7 CEV)*

After you read this devotional and pray, get up and start encouraging people. Specifically, intentionally encourage and build up 10 people you meet today.

So there's a story in the Old Testament where one day, King David sent his men to crush a rebellion that his son Absalom had started. His men fought bravely and, against all odds, crushed the rebellion. They did exactly what King David told them to do. But instead of complimenting his troops on a hard-fought battle, David complained that they took out Absalom, and he withheld any praise for his troops. Look at what general Joab told King David: If you do not start complimenting people, you surely will be a lonely person. This is more than just liking someone's Facebook post, or re-tweeting from someone's Twitter; this is using your words to compliment and encourage and be positive.

PRAYER:
Heavenly Father, thank you for the encouragement I receive from your Word. Help me to encourage 10 people today! Some of them will be right in front of me because I live with them and see them every day. Help me to affirm these special people and forgive me for taking them for granted. Other people I encourage today will be people I don't see all the time. Give me kind words that lift them up today. Help me to be intentional with my words and specific with my affirmation. Thank you that I have the power today to change someone's day and even change someone life by encouraging them. In Jesus name, Amen.

DAY 17: GET RID OF WHAT MAKES YOU NEGATIVE

Drive out the mocker, and out goes strife;
quarrels and insults are ended.
(Proverbs 22:10)

Why are you so negative? The TV or Radio you watch? Turn it off. The people you follow on social media? Unfollow. The friends you text and talk to? Get new friends. Married to the negative person? Leave them? NO! Not so fast – but do get counseling. Here is the point: we are not designed to run on negativity and cynicism.

This verse says "drive out" whatever it is that is causing conflict. How many people does it take to cause conflict? Find the negative person and kick them out of your life. You cannot hang around negative people and be positive. If you hang around complainers, you will become a complainer.

Negative blogs. There is a mocker and a complainer in all of us – insults come easy, conflict starts quickly. The best thing we can do is drive out the mocker and invite in the Master – Jesus – and say, "Jesus, come into my heart." And out goes the strife, quarrels and insults. This is a major decision you and I are going to make today – we are going to be encouragers, give compliments, and affirm others.

PRAYER:

Heavenly Father, negativity pulls my soul down. Bad news is a drain to my energy. I am beginning to see just how true it is that "words kill". Show me what is killing me. Give me discernment to identify any source of negativity – show me Lord.. Give me the courage to get rid of it – whatever it is: music, talk radio, blogs, people I follow on social media – I don't want it in my life any longer. In the same way, show me positive sources that I need more of: music, church, LifeGroup, etc. Give me wisdom to know how to guard my heart. In Jesus name, Amen.

DAY 18: BUILD UP OR TEAR DOWN

Don't use foul or abusive language. Let everything you say be good and helpful, so that your words will be an encouragement to those who hear them.
(Ephesians 4:29)

Words are like a hammer. You can build a house with a hammer. You can also tear a house down with the same hammer. Today, will you build people up or tear them down? According to Ephesians 4:29, step one is to get rid of words that aren't helpful. If the word (s) you use are not helpful, don't encourage the person you are speaking to the people who over hear them – drop those words out of your vocabulary. Ask God to guide you so that EVERYTHING you say is helpful to the other person.

So here is the filter before you say something. Six major questions:

- Is it necessary?
- Is it hurtful?
- Is it for the other person's good?
- Is it helpful?
- Is it encouraging them to be closer to God?
- Is it a blessing to anyone who hears it?

If the answer is no to ANY of these questions, <u>don't say it</u>. If the answer is yes to ALL of these questions – go ahead and build up. Anyone can tear something down, but it takes a wise person to build. Build up your family, your friends, your coworkers and classmates today.

PRAYER:
Heavenly Father, forgive me for cussing. Forgive me for using foul words that are unnecessary. Forgive me for the times I have torn down and cut down people. I want to build people around me. Help my words today and every day to be helpful. May my words cause people to look to

you and trust you. Make me an encourager. Give me the reputation of someone who is uplifting and inspiring. Let everything I say help the person I am speaking with take their next step in following You. In Jesus name, Amen.

DAY 19: SHARE THE WORD

The Lord himself will go before you. He will be with you; He will not leave you or forget you. Don't be afraid and don't worry.
(Deuteronomy 31:8)

It sounds simple. But when is the last time you shared a verse you read in the Bible with someone else? God's Word is powerful. Sometimes the best thing you can say to someone is what God said. For instance, read the verse of the day one more time. This is a great verse to share with someone.

What does this verse say? "Don't be afraid." We all need that reminder. There are 365 'don't be afraid's in the Bible – one for every day! Don't be afraid for every day of your life. Don't be afraid. Don't worry as worry blows the future out of proportion and it keeps you from enjoying the day because you are so worried about tomorrow. There is a promise we all need to and the reason why we don't have to worry: God is with us and He will never leave us or forget us.

Your assignment today: Share this verse with at least one person and see how powerful God's Word is.

PRAYER:
Heavenly Father, thank you that you yourself go before me today. Thank you that you will always be with me. Thank you that you will never leave me or forget about me. Help me to not be afraid or be worried today. I needed this encouragement from your Word today. Help me to share this verse with someone else today. I trust you. In Jesus name, Amen.

DAY 20: A HEALTHY DIET

Pleasant words are a honeycomb, sweet to the soul and healing to the bones. (Proverbs 16:24)

Do you know what honeycomb is? Honeycomb actually has more properties to help your nutrition and health than I could possibly cover here. But here are a few things:

Allergies. Chewing honeycomb for 30 minutes can stop all allergy symptoms including sneezing, runny nose and watery eyes.

Skincare. Honeycomb can be incredible for skincare

and as a facial mosturizer. It can heal scarring and many other skin infections.

Overall Benefits & Energy. Honey, especially raw, un-processed honey from a honeycomb, is said to have a pronounced effect on a body, because of honey's anti-biotic properties. It cleans the blood vessels and aids in digestion. Honey can give a person an instant energy boost.

Home Remedies. Honey has been used for many years to treat arthritis pain, sore throats, insomnia and as a natural cure for cuts and burns. This scripture is saying your words are like honeycomb. They are so powerful they can heal a sould.

Everyone around you is wounded. How are your words going to sooth and cure?

PRAYER:
Heavenly Father, help me to remember that everyone I meet today is wounded deep inside. Give me your ministry of healing with what I say. Help me to heal with my words. Make my words pleasant to your ears and others ears today. Give me the power to speak to the heart and not just the head. May my words be a source of nourishment and refreshment. In Jesus name, Amen.

DAY 21: KEEP IT GOING

Encourage one another and build each other up,
just as in fact you are doing.
(*1 Thessalonians 5:11*)

Even though this is the end of this devotional, I pray this is the beginning of a new way of speaking for you. Decide today to keep it going. Continue to read God's Word every day and speak encouraging words all day long.

This word - encourage - in Hebrew is the word Parakaleo: **Parakaleō – to give support, confidence, hope and comfort.**

The same word used to describe the Holy Spirit is the thing that we need - to come alongside each other and bring support, encouragement, hope and comfort. You know how you can do that? In the pauses. Sometimes, the best thing you can say is nothing. Expecially for those of you who just want to fix it. Maybe the best thing you can do right then is just pause and just be there. You are going to support and bring comfort and caring right now. That pause is what helps bring a peaceful quiet to the whole situation.

PRAYER:

Heavenly Father. Thank you for what you have taught me the last 21 days. You have changed my heart, which has changed my words, which has changed my relationships. This is just the beginning for me. I pledge to you this day my devotion and commitment to honor you with my words. As I have done the last 21 days, help me to do the rest of this year. Every day help me to choose to bring life, support, hope and comfort to people with my words. In Jesus name, Amen.

ABOUT THE AUTHOR

*M*ICAH DAVIDSON *is, first and foremost, a family man. He is the father of four kids and "pop" to one granddaughter. He also loves his church family. Davidson is the founder and currently the lead pastor of Real Life Church which has campuses in Corpus Christi and Austin, Texas, as well as internet viewers from 27 different countries around the world.*

He started the Corpus church with 30 families, then moved to Austin and launched the second campus in a rented house with 18 people. Real Life currently has 2,000+ who attend and who consider Real Life their home.

Davidson has trained church planters and pastors all over the world including in Africa, Central America and Eastern Europe. He has a special place in his heart for his adopted son's village in Ghana where Real Life has created life-giving water wells, held medical clinics, supported schools and started churches. Micah also develops and inspires leaders in secular fields like business, education and philanthropy. Even though he is a sought-after speaker and motivator, his favorite place is home, which is currently Austin. He loves to help people take their next step toward a better life and believes the best way to change the world is one community at a time.

Micah has a Ph.D. in Theology and his Master of Divinity with Biblical Languages from Southwestern Seminary in Ft. Worth, Texas. Only his mom calls him "Doctor," since his favorite title is "Pastor." His authentic approach to life and genuine concern for others allows Micah to connect and influence large crowds or small gatherings. His gift can be summed up by someone who recently heard him speak, "To meet him is to change; I came into this room with no hope, and now I have a new vision for my life. I will never be the same." Hopefully, you will never be the same now that you have read Micah's words and "met his heart" in this book.